by anxiety, terror, despair, and fear of rejection.

We believe that writers—both emerging and experienced—who feel supported and confident can produce their best work, and that readers benefit.

We want our readers to discover new, original works of ambitious narrative nonfiction, often by writers they are reading for the first time.

Delacorte Review | Issue 9

Michael Shapiro
Founder and Publisher

Mike Hoyt
Editor

Cissi Falligant
Senior Editor

Claire Fox
Managing Editor

Joan Hacker
Art Director

Diego Courchay
Associate Editor

Eleonore Hamelin
Illustrator

James G. Robinson
Advisor

Millie Tran
Advisor

Advisory Board
Daniel Alarcón
David Hajdu
Marguerite Holloway
Alissa Solomon
Helen Benedict
Samuel G. Freedman
LynNell Hancock
Dale Maharidge
Jonathan Weiner

Delacorte Review is published in cooperation with **Jelani Cobb**, Dean, Columbia Journalism School, and **Keith Gessen**, Director, Delacorte Center for Magazine Journalism, 2950 Broadway, New York, NY 10027. https://journalism.columbia.edu

Copyright © Delacorte Review 2023
www.delacortereview.org
ISBN 9798392928460

Contributors

Paige Bruton is a Bermudian writer, reporter and graduate student of Columbia Journalism School, specializing in long-form literary journalism, with an emphasis on first-person writing.

Maria Sole Campinoti was born and raised in Italy and pursued an undergraduate degree in History and Politics. 🐦 @solecampinoti

Hongyu (Nancy) Chen was born in China, and went to Australia for high school and university where she studied International Relations. She covers immigrant communities and senior citizens. 📷 @chen_nancyy

Isabella Anahí García-Méndez is a multimedia storyteller, reporting and producing stories in audio, video, and print. Her focus is on the intersection of business and journalism. Prior to pursuing her graduate degree, Isabella worked as a project manager in the tech industry, and graduated with a dual bachelor's degree in Political Science and French from the University of California, Berkeley. 📷 @bellaanahi

Gigi (née Giuseppe) Rajkumar Guerandi is a writer, multimedia journalist, artist, poet, musician and documentary filmmaker. Before pursuing their graduate degree, Gigi worked as a freelancer for The Daily Maverick in South Africa, in both digital and print publication, specializing in queer news and feature writing. 🐦 @giuseppeishumxn

McKenna Leavens specializes in narrative nonfiction writing and investigative reporting. She graduated with her bachelor's degree from the Walter Cronkite School of Journalism where she was the editor-in-chief of the school's fashion magazine. 🐦 @leavensmckenna

Jiayu Liang specializes in audio and environmental reporting. Before starting her master's, she worked in science communications at the Union of Concerned Scientists, an environmental and science advocacy nonprofit. 🐦 @JiayuLiang_

Contributors

Alessia Alessandra Ling de Borbon studied engineering at New York University before attending Columbia University to pursue journalism. While attending Columbia, she also works in PR and graphic design for the fashion and cosmetics industry.
✉ al4360@columbia.edu

Maria Mantas attended the University of Connecticut where she studied psychology, contributed to the UConn chapter of Her Campus, and spent her senior year working at UConn Magazine, the university's alumni publication. 🐦 @mariacmantas

Nikaline McCarley works as a freelance entertainment reporter at E! News. She previously worked at US Weekly, covering red carpets and entertainment events in New York City. 📷 @nikalinemccarley

Averee Nelson double majored in Digital Journalism and Politics & Human Rights at Marymount Manhattan College in New York City, where she was the Digital Managing Editor of the school's newspaper and an editorial intern at Her Campus Media. 🐦 @avereemar

Andrea Quezada majored in English and Communications at the University of Charleston in West Virginia. She wrote for her school's newspaper, as well as different magazines on campus.
🐦 @landreaquezada

Emma Rose is a Stabile Investigative Fellow at Columbia Journalism School and freelance reporter based in Brooklyn. She covers criminal justice stories at the intersection of social justice and human rights. She worked as a crisis response advocate for survivors of domestic and sexual violence in her hometown of Richmond, VA. 🐦 @emro_

Langchen Sun's work has experience in business reporting and data journalism. As an undergraduate in China she studied both finance and journalism. 🐦 @slangchen

Ragnhildur Thrastardottir spent four years writing and editing for Iceland's most-read newspaper, Morgunblaðið, before moving to New York to pursue a master's degree in journalism at Columbia. 🐦 @ragnhh

Mansi Vithlani specializes in long-form audio journalism, narrative nonfiction writing and investigative reporting. She has a bachelor's degree in Journalism at City, University of London, where she was also the editor-in-chief of her undergraduate magazine. 🐦 @vithlanimansi

Luwa (Elena) Yin's work has appeared in such publications as The Boston Globe and, GBH News. As an undergraduate at Boston University she produced news programs. 📷 @elena.yin

Image Attributions — **Cover, pages 6-9, 48** Photo courtesy of the author; **Page 12** Courtesy of Amy Chin and her family; **Page 18** Photo courtesy of the author; **Page 24** Photo courtesy of the author; **Page 42** Photo courtesy of the author; **Page 56** Xiang Li; **Page 66** Photo courtesy of the author; **Page 76** Northside Jim; **Page 84** Photo courtesy of the Royal Gazette; **Page 94** New York Public Library; **Page 98** Photo courtesy of the author; **Page 106** Photo courtesy of the author; **Page 124** Courtesy of the University of Alabama W.S. Hoole Special Collections Library; **Page 130** Photo courtesy of the author; **Page 138** Photo courtesy of Anna Cugnach; **Page 146** Photo courtesy of the author; **Page 158** Vigfus Sigurgeirsson.

Just Kids,

Patti Smith's best selling memoir and love letter to the late Robert Mapplethorpe, is filled with photographs. At first this seems puzzling: why would the high priestess of subversive rock and roll opt for such an easy visual device in a work of poetic non-fiction? But then again, Smith is hardly the first writer to conduct a dialogue with photographs. She's just taking us along with her.

It is in that spirit that we introduce you to seventeen photographs and the stories they tell. The stories came only after an extended period of interrogation – a dialogue in which the writers in this collection asked themselves, again and again and again: what is the story beyond this frozen moment?

The photographs themselves might seem unexceptional. Many are snapshots. Some are of men and women the writers know well, while others are of people they never met but whose stories have been passed along to them, generation after generation: a father as a teenager; an aunt captured by her estranged husband; two siblings with the brother they lost.

There is a photograph of a sonogram and another of a 19th century postcard of an asylum for the insane. There is a photo of a wedding that no one ever talked about and another of a man standing over the corpses of his wife and daughters. There is a bird taking flight. There is a woman whose smile was intended to be eternal. If pictures conceal stories, then someone must learn enough to tell them. And if pictures are moments crystalized in time, then it falls to those who have learned those stories to share them. The idea, the aspiration of this anthology, is to make the dialogue between image and the tale behind it complete.

In a world where so much is fleeting, and where we too often lose our grip on memories, we hope that this collection can be a place where memories and the stories they tell live on - for those who lived them, those who found them, and those readers who can delight in discovering them.

CONTENTS

A Door Closes. Another Opens
Hongyu (Nancy) Chen   11

His Eternal Light
Andrea Quezada   17

Sisters in Arms
Giuseppe (Gigi) Rajkumar Guerandi   23

Unfinished Business
Maria Mantas   41

The Journey to Ethan
Nikaline McCarley   47

The Reunion
Langchen Sun   55

Where Hoping Gets You
Emma Rose   65

Giving the Birds a Face
Jiayu Liang   75

A Storm Gathers on the Colony
Paige Bruton   83

The Palace of Madness
Luwa (Elena) Yin 93

Undrowning
Isabella Anahí García-Méndez 97

Letting Kishan Go
Mansi Vithlani 105

To Find a Mocking Bird
Alessia Alessandra Ling de Borbon 123

My Mother's Curse
McKenna Nicole Leavens 129

An Unexpected Friendship in Times of War
Maria Sole Campinoti 137

A Portrait of my Imperfect Father
Averee Nelson 145

The Daughter Who Lived
Ragnhildur Thrastardottir 157

A DOOR CLOSES.
ANOTHER OPENS

Hongyu (Nancy) Chen

The father folding the shirt was the owner of this laundry. The daughter, who was two, was keeping him company. Despite the father having a successful business, the daughter would not take over. This made the father pleased.

The father, Pang Fook Chin, was 37 years old in August 1964 when the photo was taken. He was proud of this laundry. In fact, he owned two others in the Bronx. They were among the most profitable in the entire borough, representing the success of the family that had been here since the late 19th century. Pang Fook's grandfather arrived from China to work building a railroad. His father ran a laundry. The path that led Pang Fook here would stop with him. He is the end of one era. His daughter is the beginning of another.

The story of how Pang Fook came to be the last in his family to own a laundry began in Guangdong, a province in southeast China. In the mid-to-late 19th century, people there started hearing about the Gold Mountain – a place where they could make their fortune

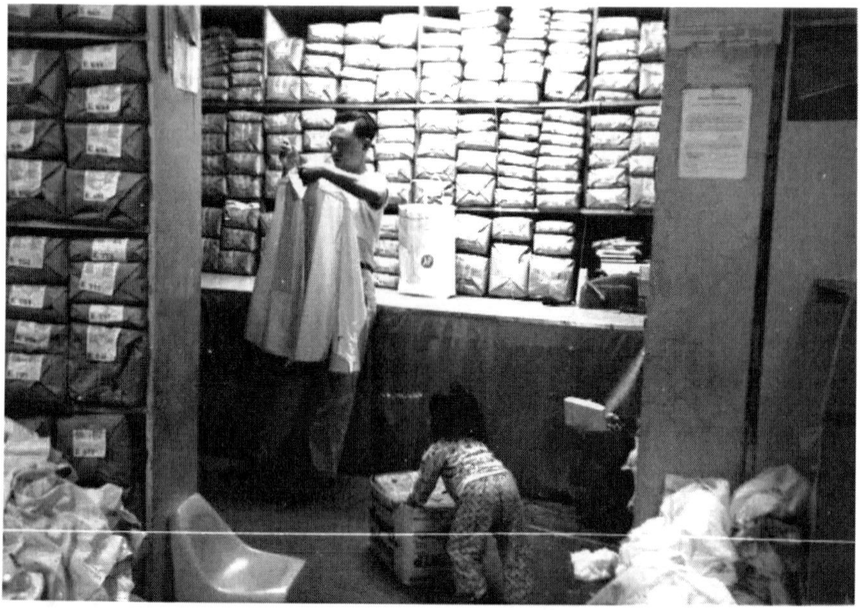

and return with so much money they could build fancy houses and hire servants. The Gold Mountain was located on the other side of the Pacific Ocean – the United States.

But as more and more Chinese people arrived at the Gold Mountain, they soon realized that they were not welcome. The increasing number of Chinese laborers threatened non-Chinese workers, who believed the foreigners would drive down wages and squeeze them out of jobs.

To make matters worse, in 1882 Congress passed the Chinese Exclusion Act. The Act forbade Chinese laborers from entering the country for 10 years and prohibited them from becoming U.S. citizens. The only exemptions included diplomats, students, teachers, merchants and travelers. It marked the first restrictive immigration law in the U.S. and was made indefinite in 1904 before finally being repealed in 1943.

The Act made the journey for Chinese people wanting to come to the U.S. very difficult. So they had to seek creative ways to get around these restrictions. The 1906 San Francisco earthquake provided them with an opportunity. The fires that burned for three days destroyed the city, including records and documents like birth certificates. Many Chinese citizens then claimed that they were U.S.-born and that their documents were lost in the fire.

Pang Fook's father, Bok Ying Chin, was one of them.

Bok Ying arrived in Seattle in August 1913 and claimed he was from Napa, California. He boarded a train to New York and settled down in Chinatown, where he worked in a laundry.

Being a laundryman was very common for Chinese men back then. Discrimination and harassment against the Chinese were institutionalized. They were not allowed to work at any level of the government and were prohibited from sending their children to public schools. They were beaten, robbed and sometimes killed. The Chinese found little help from the government.

Domestic work, like washing clothes, was considered dirty and tiresome so the Chinese saw an opportunity. An immigrant named Wah Lee opened the first Chinese laundry in San Francisco in 1851. He charged $5 to wash a dozen items. The business was booming within weeks. He soon employed 20 people and operated three shifts a day. Then he had competitors.

By the early 1900s, roughly one in four Chinese men worked in a laundry. They worked 10 to 16 hours a day to make enough money to send to their families back home. By the 1930s, there were as many as 3,000 Chinese laundry workers in New York.

But even in the laundry industry, the Chinese still faced discrimination. In San Francisco, for example, laws were passed that required laundries to be operated only in brick buildings. Out of the 320 laundries in the city, 310 were located in wooden buildings. The Chinese owned 240 of them. Non-Chinese laundries were mostly granted permits to operate in wooden buildings but hardly any Chinese laundries were granted the same permits.

On the east coast, non-U.S. citizens were not allowed to own washing machinery. Therefore, they needed to send the dirty laundry to washing companies, often owned by white people. Laundry workers in New York established the Chinese Hand Laundry Alliance in 1933.

Over the years, Bok Ying was able to save enough money to pay for several trips going back and forth to China. He also got a "paper son," Pang Ngip.

"Paper son" was another creative way for Chinese people to come to the U.S. – a system of using fake documents to "prove" that they were descendants of Chinese people already living in the U.S. Many paper sons changed their names to align with their "paper fathers."

Despite the legal obstacles, roughly 175,000 Chinese people passed through Angel Island in San Francisco Bay between 1910 and 1940, according to the Library of Congress.

Pang Fook, the third child of Bok Ying, fled to Hong Kong with his wife, Linda Moy Chin, after the Chinese Civil War. He left Linda behind when he went to the U.S. in 1951. He was detained and interrogated at Ellis Island for three months before being allowed into the country. He then went to work at his father's laundry. The family was separated for nine years before Pang Fook had saved enough money to bring them to the U.S. A year later, his daughter Lily was born. Amy was born the year after.

The family's first laundry in the Bronx was destroyed in a fire in the late 1950s. They then bought a new one. Across the front window were the words "PANG F. CHIN HAND LAUNDRY."

The laundry was small. But the front felt spacious to little Amy – big enough to play with her siblings and ride her tricycle. The back was separated by a curtain, and that was where the family lived. There was a kitchen, a bed squeezed in, and a table where they ate and where the kids did their homework. Amy also had friends over for birthday parties.

The laundry usually opened at 8 a.m. and stayed open until late at night. The family later bought their own house in nearby Parkchester. When business got very busy, Pang Fook would sleep in the back of the laundry.

Amy came home for lunch at the laundry when she was in elementary school. Her parents would temporarily close the laundry, pick her up and bring her home. As Amy grew older, she went to junior high school with Robert Levinson, whose parents were longtime customers of the Chin's laundry. In fact, Mrs. Levinson and Mrs. Chin already knew each other when they were pregnant. They even compared their pregnancy journeys. Amy's and Robert's birthdays were one month apart.

When he was in junior high school, Robert hung out in the laundry. He liked to stand behind the counter and greet customers. Pang Fook would let him pass on the packages to the customers and occasionally let him try to wrap the packages. Although Robert never thought he was good at packaging, he felt his presence was a source of amusement to Amy and Lily. He recalls that when the customers saw him – a tall, white boy – standing behind the counter, they would make fun of him with a friendly smirk. Robert remembers that the laundry was so organized that Amy's parents always knew exactly where to find each customer's package.

Sunday for Amy was the "best" day of the week. The family often gave themselves a treat and went to Chinatown for Dim Sum. Other times, her parents would close the store and invite their Chinese friends to play mahjong.

By the 1960s and 70s, Chinese laundry businesses were in decline.

The dry-cleaning industry was growing and as synthetic fabrics got increasingly popular, people no longer needed pressed shirts as they had before.

Meanwhile, Amy went to the prestigious Bronx High School of Science. She still helped out at the laundry but it became less frequent once she enrolled at Barnard.

Her father continued to work at the laundry until his death in 1988. He was 60. None of his four children took over the laundry, nor did he want them to. The family sold the business to an outsider who told Amy's mother, "I will build it back to its former glory." The laundry, however, closed in the year 2000.

Amy graduated with a degree in East Asian Studies. After her mother died in 2006, the children went through the things she and Pang Fook left behind and began retracing their roots. Like many families, the Chins decided to put their story into a book. But instead of telling their story using words alone, the Chin family told it in the form of a graphic novel. It traces the family's story from the arrival of the great grandfather who worked on the railroad up to Amy, who became a researcher and board president of Think!Chinatown, a community organization.

A few years ago, Amy returned to the Bronx to see what had become of the laundry her father owned. The laundry was gone. In its place was a restaurant. It was small and that reminded her of what it had been like to grow up in the laundry which had felt so big when she was young.

HIS ETERNAL LIGHT

Andrea Quezada

It is impossible not to notice the portrait of my *abuela* in my grandfather's home. It hangs in the family living room. The colors are bright, especially set against the white wall where it hangs, and because the light above it is forever illuminated.

My grandfather commissioned the portrait after my *abuela* died. He gave the artist two photographs to work from. One photograph is the primary inspiration, but for my grandfather, it lacked something essential: a smile. So, he instructed the artist to use the smile from the second photograph. He also asked the artist to make smaller versions so that his children could have a similar portrait in their homes.

My grandma, known to everyone else as Rosa Maria and as *abuela*

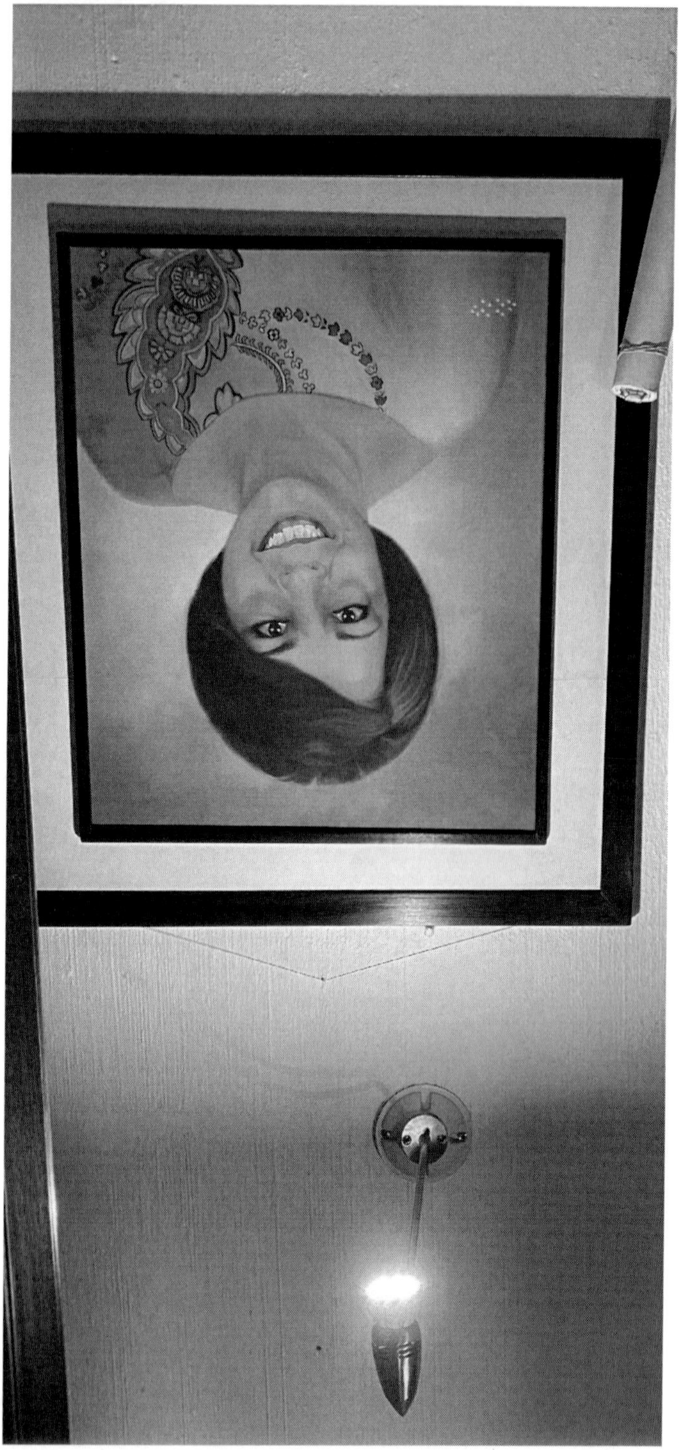

to me, was born in August 1946 in Guatemala. Though she was intelligent, she was not the most studious or responsible student in school. She would often skip classes or when she was in class, she was easily distracted by something other than the lecture. She was, however, always the first one to volunteer as an organizer for events – during and after school. She liked to host them at her house.

My *abuela* liked to tease. One time she challenged a friend to eat as many pieces of cake as she could, daring her to eat more than six. Her friend ate all the slices she could. Then she got sick – as my *abuela* knew she would.

She was a child of privilege. Her father owned a coffee farm and the family was prosperous, especially compared to the poverty around them. My uncles went into the family business and while I had wondered whether my *abuela* felt thwarted not to be a part of the family enterprise, her friend assured me that she was content in the role of being her father's personal assistant for a different business.

When she was still a teenager – perhaps 16 or 17 – her father bought a car and it was as she was driving that car that my grandfather first noticed her.

He was hanging out at a friend's house when he saw her drive up. When she rolled down the window and waved he noticed she was wearing white gloves. He asked his friends who she was. She's our cousin, they said. He was interested; they were the same age. They told him she was out of his league. He should not even try to flirt with her.

My grandfather, however, was undeterred. My *abuela's* cousin told him that if in six months he could get her to be his girlfriend, he would buy a round of drinks. My grandfather agreed but said that he only needed 30 days for her to agree to be his girlfriend. And with that, he started pursuing her.

It took him 28 days. They would remain a couple for the rest of her life.

My grandfather became a lawyer and my *abuela* did start working for her dad's company. They both spent long days in the office and long nights having fun with their friends. Eventually, they got married and had three children.

HIS ETERNAL LIGHT 19

My *abuela* stopped working. My grandfather's circle of friends and business associates grew. Together, they would go out for the evening or have people over. They traveled to Europe and the United States. He got along well with her family. They spent weekends with their children. Their lives were full and happy.

But then in her early 50s, my *abuela* was diagnosed with multiple sclerosis. She began to have difficulty walking. The evenings out were less and less frequent. The trips to America were to visit doctors in Miami. She tried her best to carry on as she always had. But there were days in which her legs would give out or she would be too tired to get out of bed. She still hosted friends when she felt well enough.

She became a grandmother. I would visit her on weekends and we would read books together. We laughed a lot. She did not lose her smile. The treatments, however, took over more of her life.

In May of 2011, she was admitted to the hospital for what I assumed by now was another routine medical procedure. It was not. There was a problem with her colon and to this day I do not know the specifics. She died in her sleep a month later. She was 65.

My grandfather began working less and less and spending more time at home alone. He stopped seeing many of his friends and started watching movies and sports on TV. He stopped traveling. He avoided the places that reminded him of my *abuela*.

Less than a year after her death my grandfather commissioned the painting. He knew a couple who were both artists. The husband had done a posthumous portrait of my *abuela's* parents. He asked the wife if she would paint a portrait of my *abuela*. She agreed and asked for photographs to work from.

My grandfather could not settle on a photo. There were some in which she looked lovely but something was missing. There were others in which she was smiling but was not positioned in a way that flattered her.

He decided on a photo taken during our last family vacation the year before her death, in which she was posing for the photographer. Yet her smile was not the one that he wanted in the painting. So he sent the artist a second photo with her smiling.

After my grandfather saw the portrait he knew he had chosen

well, in both the pictures and the painter. He felt she had captured his wife.

As the years have passed, the void that my *abuela* left in my grandfather's life remains. There is a sadness to him, even when he tries to be happy. On special occasions he will say "I wish she was here" or "she should be here."

Every morning when he gets out of bed and walks into the living room he sees the portrait. It is always illuminated and she is always smiling at him.

SISTERS IN ARMS

Giuseppe (Gigi) Rajkumar Guerandi

It feels like there's been a Vijay-shaped hole in my family's collective heart that's been bleeding on everything for 22 years. In fact, few things reduce my mother to a tall child quite like the subject of her late sister.

Each year on her death day, September 14, Ma roams the house in a grief-stricken stupor. Alone, she wails, drinks, and communes with the ghost of her sister. Like a harbinger of the end that never left, a banshee hung up on an old death. The overblown photo of Vijay on her twenty-first birthday hovers over the whole house, the cloud of her Mona Lisa smile — perfectly trapped in a gold frame — looms larger than usual on that great sad day. Look into her eyes long enough and you'd swear she knew she had already spent two-thirds of her life.

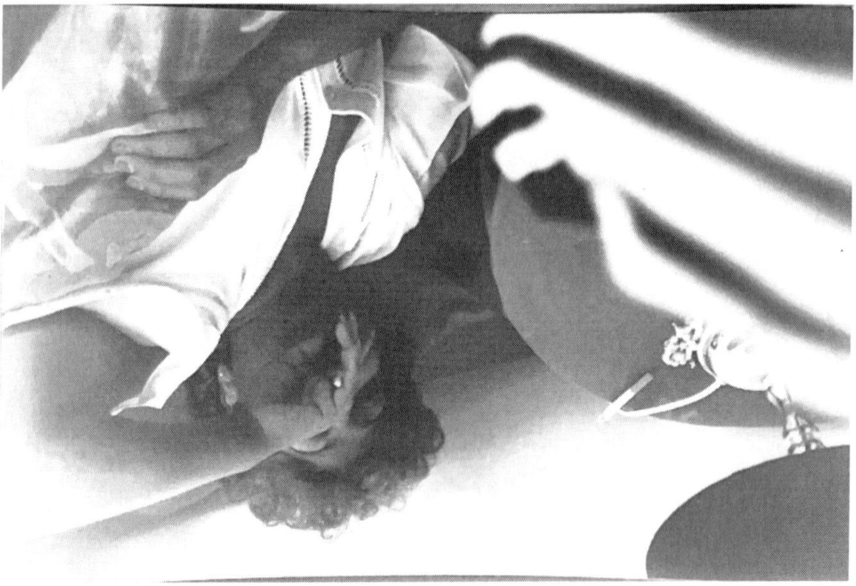

In our grand tradition, Ma sets a thimble of milk and a shot of brandy at the foot of the photo she has propped on the dining room table. A plate of food, typically a piping hot *sabzi* or *briyani* dish, is placed in front of this altar for her to feast, our token of respect to the deceased. Opium incense sticks burn, shedding onto a mountain of accumulating ash. Ma mutters as the day progresses, increasingly drunk on mourning. She seemingly pleads with the void, and if you listen closely you can make out the faintest demanding question: "Why did you go?"

The whole scene unfolds like the saddest séance, an ill-fated ritual to resurrect what cannot be. I would be frightened if I wasn't so used to it.

You see, with no intention of diminishing whatever pain you carry, my friend, no one grieves like my family grieves. Worse still, no family leaves wounds untreated the way my family will fester and bleed out. In the vein of Indian mythology, I know Vijay through an inter-generational anthology that my family raised me on.

But why tell stories of a godmother I never knew? And at what cost did we tell them? As it turns out, no good story goes unpunished, and I never really knew Vijay at all.

The photo you see was taken by Ma in a moment of spontaneous and accidental artistry. Vijay is pictured in her mother-in-law's home, a woman she used to call "that cock-eyed fucking bitch," according to Ma. The figure standing over Vijay is her husband, Shan, a man Ma calls "that asshole." A lone cigarette with no ashtray to hang it in burns dangerously on the edge of the bedside table. Its neighbor is a rosary, befitting a woman of unwavering faith.

I'll tell you what I know about Vijay. She was the eldest of five children — three sisters and two brothers. They were born and raised in extreme poverty in the heart of the province of KwaZulu-Natal in South Africa, moving around from townships and shanty houses because of their father's erratic employment status. Their mother, Big Ama, was an uneducated housewife with the kindest smile I've ever seen in photo. She comes to me in my dreams some nights or places a hand on my shoulder when I'm standing over a pot of chicken curry, desperately trying and perpetually falling short of capturing the magic of that generational recipe. Their father, Big Daddy, was a more difficult man to grapple with. He battled a savage alcoholism and routinely beat his wife and children. I've never dreamt of him.

These are some tales of Vijay I can recite from memory at this point: While waiting for the truck that she and her siblings hitched a ride home from school, she'd climb a nearby Doni tree to pick its fruit for her siblings, who were starving by that point in the day. After all, a little tomato chutney on bread can hardly sustain a child through the school day, on the rare occasion they had even that.

She would steal relentlessly where she could, either by bullying the other six-year-old girls on the bus or pilfering a few ice creams from a tuck shop on a hot summer's day, though they would melt to a puddly mess in a soggy pocket by the time she got them to her siblings.

My favorite story of Vijay is the one where she did her darndest to uphold the social status of her siblings. The most popular sweets in school at the time were Sparkles, petite crystalline jewels of sugary goodness and fluorescent colors. They couldn't afford the prized little gems, so Vijay rummaged through the dumpsters by their school, found some discarded beer bottles, and shattered them on the gravel into little pseudo-candies. She handed the shards of glass to her siblings to suck on in front of their classmates, mouths cut up and bleeding, but embarrassment spared. She was eight years old.

An imaginary word from my family is "Atha," which translates to aunt. This word comes courtesy of Vijay herself, who invented it for me.

"Where's Atha's boy?" she would call to me first thing in the morning, in her house in coastal Richards Bay on the weekends my parents and I would visit. I was only a few months old then, but I'm told she would scoop me up from my cot at the crack of dawn and tuck me in bed between her and her husband until my parents eventually came to collect me. This became somewhat of a routine in those early weeks of my life, when my parents made the trip to her place regularly.

I'm not a boy anymore, but I wish I could remember the sound of her hushed voice ringing down the hall, playfully starting my day with that mischievous siren indicating an incoming heist: *"Where's Atha's boy?"* Unfortunately I can't hear it, despite my best efforts to wrack the recesses of my mind, but I'd like to believe it's true. I'm told she loved me, and that I believe.

Shortly after that, the cancer quickly gripped her and didn't let go until it had ravaged her body entirely. Toward the end, Ma spent "seven days and seven nights" taking care of her as a de facto live-in nurse. She would read Vijay the Bible passage from Psalm 23 when she could muster the request and feed her my baby porridge, the only thing she could stomach at 3 in the morning when the faintest sign of her appetite would emerge.

Then, she died at 34, taken suddenly and excruciatingly by breast cancer.

"I was her baby," Ma says, in reference to being the youngest of five, but with an infantile earnestness that would make you forget it was not Vijay's hips that cracked to thrust her into this world. No, that would be Big Ama, and she was already gone by the time we lost Vijay. In fact, both Big Ama and Big Daddy were dead by 1997.

For Ma, raising me on these stories was partly a way of atoning for the fact that she couldn't save her sister. A debt for the sacrifices Vijay had made to make her the woman she is today.

Ma says, "I think she knew that I was supposed to take her place when she died."

Ma's favorite memories of Vijay are the tainted ones, where she was saving them from something. One time, when Ma was no more than eight or nine years old, her yellow dress brushed against Big Daddy's glass and knocked his drink over. He wanted to beat her, but Vijay grabbed her tiny hand and ran with her out onto the main road until he gave up chasing them.

Another time, for her first school trip, Ma's class was going on an excursion to Five Mile Beach, and was required to wear jeans and a t-shirt. She had never owned a pair of jeans in her life. Ma still doesn't know how she did it, but when she got home from school one afternoon leading up to the day of the outing, Vijay came home from work with a brand new pair of stone-washed jeans and a pink shirt.

Whether she had begged, borrowed or stolen is unclear and irrelevant, because Vijay was her good fairy at that moment. Vijay herself always had holes in her worn panties for most of her life.

My remaining aunt, Jeeva, is a piece of work. She's the middle of the three sisters, and the second-born of the five siblings. At 56, she's survived a stroke, a heart attack, triple bypass surgery and Covid-19. She smoked like a chimney, although I'm not sure how appropriate the past tense is in this case, and drank like a sailor, the tense of which is slightly more plausible. She tells stories in theatrical extremes worthy of the amphitheaters of ancient Rome.

Jeev's happiest moments with Vijay were those pockets of time they spent just sitting together, staying up into the wee hours of the night to talk about each other and everything going on in their lives. Just two young girls sharing a bed and laughing about nothing, at things that "didn't even matter" when everything around them mattered most.

By the time Ma was born, Vijay had to grow up. Vijay was nine and they were tested once more. Big Daddy was thrown in jail for drunkenly assaulting someone. As bad luck would have it, at that same moment Big Ama endured severe burns from the primus burner they cooked on, and had to be hospitalized. The extended family either refused or could not take in the five parentless children, so they took care of themselves under the guidance of their nine-year-old elder.

Vijay ordered her three younger siblings to work for the landlord in the fields, cutting green beans and whatever else was ready to be harvested. She would lock Ma, barely a toddler, in the house and ask the neighbor to keep an intermittent eye on the baby through a window. Then, she'd make her way on foot to a nearby shop to make bread for the aunty that worked there. As Indians, we call all older women "aunty" as a sign of respect.

Make no mistake, the kids all went to school; Vijay made sure of it. They'd rush in the mornings and climb under the wire fence behind the school to sneak in on time, like covert child soldiers. When the school day was done they'd head to their respective employers.

At the end of her workday, the aunty would give Vijay the leftover ingredients as groceries, like a half-full bottle of oil and scraps of chili powder. Vijay also begged the aunty for whatever money she could spare to buy bread, margarine and the like. According to Jeev, this was how her big sister sustained their small battalion.

Despite Ma's young age, this period is the source of her earliest conscious memories. She can still vividly see the yellow police van taking Big Daddy away. She remembers being the first one bathed when the other siblings returned home, and the first one fed and put to bed at the behest of Vijay. She'd carry 20-liter drums of water on her head up the hill to boil for bathing her siblings.

Vijay dropped out of school just before high school. She was the best at math and science, but Big Daddy couldn't afford to put everyone through high school, so Vijay sacrificed to ensure the rest could. Nonetheless, she eventually became a "self-made accountant," faking her way on sheer smarts and adaptation.

At the time her teacher, Mr. Naidoo, even drove into the bushland where they lived, in an area they called Cactus, to beg Big Daddy to keep Vijay in school. Without much choice, he refused.

"Vijay was never one to show emotions," Ma says. "But that broke her."

Her first job was at a place called Hillestad, working as a cashier. It was a kind of inventory grocery store where people went to bulk buy and stock up on essentials. She was 13 years old.

She was never happy there. She was a go-getter who needed more power over her situation, so her next place of employment was Power Stores in an area called Empangeni — a bad joke courtesy of Ma. She was around 15 by then, but Big Daddy still wasn't financially coping, even with Vijay's salary. That's when he took Jeev out of school to help out.

Jeev worked a receptionist job that Vijay had got for her, about a kilometer away from her own workplace. They'd hitchhike to work, and if they were lucky the boss would drop them off at home afterward. They'd always share lunch breaks together at Vijay.

In her job, Jeev was always putting the calls through to every office except the right one, because she'd never touched a switchboard in her life. Every lunch she'd run down to Vijay's office, where she'd already be cooking something up in the microwave. Jeev would cry to her about how she's messing up and the boss is cussing her out. Vijay would tell her, "You understand you want to be in the big world. In order for you to be working, it's going to be a rough patch. You've got to start learning to use your intuition and what you have to do. People cannot tell you what you have to do."

That's when Jeev started realizing that if she wanted to be in the big world, she'd have to start acting and doing things like big people do. She could not be a teenager anymore. Then they would have a smoke, and Jeev would run back to her workplace. Vijay would pick her up in the afternoon, and they'd go home.

During this time, the brothers and Ma used to take the school bus in the mornings, which made a stop nearby Jeev's workplace. She would purloin a few Fantas and savory hot pies from the bakery nearby and sneak them through the school bus window to her ravenous young siblings.

Ma says with a pained chuckle, "I've never been more proud of theft."

This only lasted about three months. Then Jeev went back to school and graduated. When Vijay found Jeev's next job, this time at Delta Motors, it was 10 kilometers away from her.

"I couldn't run to her every lunch break," she laments. "I had to carry my own lunch now, getting a little independent."

Vijay worked doubly hard at the cashiering gig, faked experience to get a bookkeeping job by 19, and with that paycheck she got her siblings through school.

"She got the end of the stick, and that was it," as Jeev puts it, in her unintentionally profound way. After that, Jeev joined the police force in 1988, in the child protection unit.

"We shouted at each other, but never put a slap for each other," remembers Jeev. "The time we disagreed, tragedy fell."

One such tragedy was a car accident fueled by liquor, in which Jeev sustained a considerable neck fracture that affects her to this day. Ma was in the car too, and she would tell me how Vijay lost a part of her nose from the impact.

Even speaking now, Jeev looks up to her lost sister, because of how she worked around the situation they were placed in. She also knows that Vijay was never someone to go to somebody and ask for help.

Ma confirms this. Vijay had a strong exterior always, and processed anything beyond the moment, but that rockhard facade was fickle. "She was the saddest, most broken person," Ma says. It was in those quiet, fleeting moments when she'd be sitting by herself that Ma could glimpse the well of sadness in Vijay's eyes. Ma was caught up in growing up, unable to do anything to change it.

"We could never love the way she loved — unconditionally — her brothers and sisters, her parents," says Jeev. "That part of her life I cannot give, I cannot expect, I cannot share. It's all over now for us."

In the end, Vijay spiraled the annals of a gambling addiction, laying her life down on a blackjack table.

"She made use of her money in a bad way, but she enjoyed herself, and I'm glad she did," says Jeev. "I never knew that brought her joy; to me, it was just like she wasted her life away."

I call my father Pops. He knew Vijay briefly. My parents got married in November of 1998 after knowing each other for a few short months, and she was gone by 2001. And yet, if there's one thing the women on my Indian side can agree on, it's that Pops and Vijay got on like a house on fire.

"It was short and sweet," he says.

On the surface, this Indian woman and Italian man couldn't appear more different. Vijay smoked, where Pops detests the stuff. Vijay had an affinity for brandy, where Pops can barely stand the smell of it. Vijay was an insatiable gambler, where Pops always left the casino first. And yet, Ma recalls with fondness to this day how Vijay was the only person alive who could get my father to drink a smidge of brandy with her.

The way Pops tells it, what forged their connection so quickly and deeply were their shared values. To him, they seemed to view the world in a similar way, knowing how things ought to be, at least to them. She couldn't live out those values in her own life, and he recognized that, but it was clear to him she wanted to. She wished she could. To this day he admires her intelligence, and ability to lead her familial troop.

It was New Year's Day of 2000, before Vijay returned home to Richards Bay from Johannesburg, that Ma asked Pops to have a look at the lump on the outer side of her sister's breast. He knew immediately. The growth that she often joked was a third nipple was more akin to a bulbous mass.

For reasons I can only postulate, Vijay heeded his warning and saw a doctor. It was a Monday, ten days into that new millennium, when Ma got the call from her big sister. It was stage four breast cancer. Vijay was devastated.

The mass on her breast had been growing for years, so why didn't she get it checked out sooner? Pops chalks it up to a self-destructiveness he saw in her. Much like Ma, Vijay had a debilitating fear of going to the doctor. A kind of underlying knowing of the worst that could only be kept at bay without medical confirmation. She was also just petrified of what she saw as the mutilation of her body if her worst fears were indeed true.

Perhaps Ma doesn't share this phobia with Vijay, but acquired it from her. Either way, Ma argues that Vijay was simply tired.

For Vijay, nobody stood by her the way Big Daddy did, and when he died she fell like a china doll from a great height and shattered. She was 30, just four years away from her own demise, and without him, the world could take advantage of her. That's when her husband's affair started, and she let it happen. This was her nadir.

My eldest cousin is Natasha – Natty – Vijay's firstborn. She handles her tequila better than any man you've ever known, and her shimmering sari is the one my mind's eye clings to most from Diwalis past.

Within two years of Big Daddy's death, Vijay attempted suicide three times before the cancer took her. Pills were her method. Natty was always there, and Jeev had to intervene every time. Natty would call her in Durban to come back. Vijay was saved every time, but she'd still telephone Ma in her office in Joburg and cry, saying she couldn't do this anymore.

"Without Natty," Ma says, "Vijay would've died much sooner."

Natty took care of me while Ma took care of Vijay in her final days. Ma had to monitor Vijay's oxygen and morphine, keeping her environment as sterile as a hospital. Vijay chose to suffer in silence until she died, even when it became too painful to verbalize what she felt.

The first time Ma ever saw Vijay struck by Big Daddy, truly beaten, was when he caught Vijay talking to a boy in the park at the age of 15. Ma was only seven at the time, but she can still hear Vijay's scream through her parents' bedroom door. Ma can barely bring herself to call the young man Vijay's boyfriend, it was so nascent, but that didn't matter to their patriarch.

His weapon of choice was a *sjambok*, a kind of South African leather whip, girthy in its unbreakable fibers and devastating enough to leave craters where it met with flesh. Ma can never forget Vijay's bludgeoned eye.

Big Daddy was strange in his outlook on women. Ma boils it down to our cultural mores, at least of that time, where a girl child couldn't be caught talking to boys, dressing "inappropriately," or even "reading a romance book," to use Ma's example. She recalls a common threat of her father's, that if he ever caught any of his three girls behaving in these grossly romantic or sexual manners he'd "put our heads on the doorstep and cut our necks off."

At the same time, Big Daddy only had time for his three girls, and none whatsoever for his two boys. By Ma's description, he believed that his boys were stupid and destined to be their uneducated mother's problem, while his three girls would be intelligent successes that he would keep in line. I'm not sure that there can be a definitive psycho-feminist take on my late grandfather's rationale, but his children certainly suffered for it. Yet even still, Big Daddy was the marrow in Vijay's bones.

Natty was 18 when her mother died.

Her favorite memory of her mother was when she taught her how to make fish *briyani* just before she died. She was too sick to get up and go to the kitchen and stand over a stovetop. So she sat down at the dining room table and dictated the process step-by-step. It turned out great, but nothing like if she'd made it herself.

"Nothing will ever taste like her food," she says. "When you speak of your mom, you speak of the best."

Natty's worst memories are the fist fights on the weekends.

Weekends were about partying and drinking and the family was in their own little world. The children dreaded the weekends. That weekly rotation of picking at old, barely-sealed scabs and fresh, new wounds. Liquor can be like a key for our family it seems, knocking down our thinly-veiled walls and unlocking our barely-there boundaries to finally address the things we cannot bring ourselves to confront by day.

Neel, Natty's husband, mentioned his suspicions of the affair to Vijay, but she chose not to see it most of the time. However, Natty can recall the nights her mother would muster up the liquid courage to point out the less-than-clandestine affair her husband was having with her sister-in-law, trying to taunt an admission of guilt out of them. Shan, her husband at the time, took all of her clothes and threw them on the floor in the passage, setting the pile of fabric ablaze. Everything in the house was broken. Natty was 15, but this had been a mainstay of those weekends long before then. Vijay had to just sit there and watch to avoid being struck.

Natty remembers that marriage as violent. After a bout of abuse, her mother would just stay holed up in her room. All Natty could do was scream, run and take cover. Vijay never spoke to Natty about it, but she had a lot of time for Jeeva, and spoke to her about a lot of this hell.

Natty also remembers, in no uncertain terms, the night her mother's eldest brother raised his hand up to Vijay too, after she picked on his wife and voiced her disdain for her family. He inherited a lot of violence and contributed it to these fights. That was when he climbed on top of her cancerous body, strangling her on her marital bed.

Natty is precise and unwavering in her descriptions, the kind of clinical recounting of trauma that I've seen from so many of the children in our family. She just stood there, screaming, pleading with this man to get off her mother. She was helpless, she was afraid, and she knew if she tried to intervene the next hand would be laid on her.

The next morning the adults awoke from their destruction, shook off the calamities of the previous night, and continued with the day to nurse their hangovers on the beach, unfazed until the following weekend. In this house we don't wipe our slates clean, we pile onto them indefinitely.

Natty resented her mother sometimes. She wished she'd spent more time with her children. If she had money, that's how she supplemented love. She'd spend more time with her siblings than them. It was always about them. As Ma puts it, Vijay was a prisoner in her own family.

"I wish I could've spent more time with her," Natty says. "I wish she would've spent more time with me."

Jeev knows this to be true, and doesn't shy away from it. "If her brother had nothing to eat, believe you me she would make sure he had something to eat. But if her children had nothing to eat, she'll probably let them go to sleep without food. But then you look at it, children go through worse…They can get over a situation."

Natty wasn't there when her mother died. She was working. Neel picked her up from work and his first words were, "She's gone." Natty felt sick that morning and almost didn't go to work, but pushed through and did so anyway. She would regret that. Neel just hugged her but she didn't know how to react or feel. She remembers she couldn't bring herself to look at her mother when she arrived at the family home where she had died. They had her laid on the sofa with the blanket over her.

Natty says, "I always thought that someday she'd walk through the door."

Her earliest memory is when her dad left at age two. She can remember him leaving. She was standing in her petite dress on the front seat of the car. "I haven't seen him since, 38 years later." Vijay never spoke of him again. "He was forgotten."

Sixteen members of the family lived under the same roof before Vijay bought a house, but Natty spent more time with Big Ama and Big Daddy. They sold vegetables for a living. They'd go to the market on Friday nights and come back on Saturdays. She remembers the blue packet of ladyfingers they'd bring back for her. But the night before there'd be alcohol and problems, and it wasn't suddenly rosy with them either — Big Daddy was still as abusive as ever, and Big Ama got a beating until the day he lost her. Nonetheless, they were her stand-in parents while Vijay oversaw the whole family.

Then Big Ama died in 1996 of a heart attack. Eleven months later, Big Daddy died of a broken heart.

Natty was with them when Big Ama had the heart attack. It was a Saturday and they were on the beach. When they got home, she insisted on having a hot bath and her cup of milky tea, the kind where the cream rose to the top. Then the chest pain overwhelmed her.

Natty remembers her in the hospital, in her hospital gown. She couldn't speak. Then the next thing she remembers was Vijay running out the door. She was screaming and made for the road, ready to throw herself into oncoming traffic.

"We had to grab her," Natty says. "She couldn't handle it." There was an unspoken understanding of the shared abuse they were put through, and losing Big Ama meant losing an ally.

"I somehow think she had a premonition of our parents dying early," says Jeev.

Big Daddy went downhill almost immediately, circling the drain faster every day without his wife. He died of depression. Without fail, he'd go to her grave daily to have a cup of tea with her over his morning newspaper. He'd share meals with her, leaving food for her spirit.

Natty believes that what Ma went through with Vijay is what Vijay went through with Big Daddy. Watching them die right in front of them. He wasn't eating properly, but there was one day he asked for food. He was craving KFC; he was nearing the end and he knew it.

"Everyone wants to remember the good about their parents, but there's also bad to them," Natty says. "Mom was no angel. Yes, there were things she did wrong in her life, but at the end of the day she's still my mom. No matter what they do, they're still the best."

Vijay endured half of her cancer journey with Ma on the ragged plot of land in Johannesburg we lived on, where Pops still resides today. Our quarters were the round walls of a mud hut on that land, adorned with a thatch roof and a dirty cream-colored exterior. This was during the radiation and chemotherapy process, when I was barely a year old. Jeev had to come down from Durban to help care for her and me while Ma and Pops went to work everyday.

Vijay and I were at two very different stages of our lives then, and

36 SISTERS IN ARMS

as hers waned mine began. We were experiencing the vulnerability of small babies in need of care, but from polar opposite ends of that spectrum.

My favorite story that Ma and Jeev told me of that time is rather dark, as I was by all accounts a taunting toddler with a twisted sense of humor. When the chemo inevitably led to hair loss, I took up the sadistic habit of sneaking up on Vijay with my unstable but light-footed waddle, to pull out small fistfuls of her thinning locks. Vijay had beautiful curls, reminiscent of mine in photos at age three. I lost mine with time, she lost hers to me.

Vijay's three children all had different fathers. Natty is Jeffrey's daughter. Ashleigh is Rajan's son. Leanne is Shan's daughter. Ma was eight years old when Vijay brought Jeffrey into their lives. He would be Ma's first rapist.

The first time it happened, Ma just looked at the ceiling with laser focus, trying her best to dissociate from her child's body and what was being done to it. At that moment she dreamed a dream. She dreamed of me.

When he was finished, he delivered her back to Vijay at Gary's Cafe. They walked together on the dirt road in silence. Blood was trailing down her legs. She struggled to walk. She was in pain.

I don't know if she was too callous to see or too cruel to accept it, but Vijay didn't take notice. She did nothing. By the time she was with Rajan, Ma was motivated by a resolve and her newfound faith in God to come out with the truth to Vijay about Jeffrey. She was not believed.

Vijay called her a "trouble-causer," "a liar." Ma herself started to believe she made the whole thing up. She wanted her big sister to hold her, to tell her it would be okay and that she was there and nobody would hurt her again. Instead, Ma carried the truth of her first rapist, and every one after him, alone for most of her life.

"Of course I resent her, it was an ugly part of her," Ma says. "There is so much abuse with the men she brought into our house." For Ma, she was the baby, and nobody saw how that baby was getting abused for 12 years.

Vijay's taste in men was less than desirable, and around every corner of them was a betrayal. Jeffrey was raping Ma. Jeev and Rajan had a brief affair. Shan and her sister-in-law fooled around even as she lay on her deathbed. She wanted to be loved, to put her love in a man she could trust. It was her most basic need, and her most damaging blindspot.

I'm not sure that you're meant to *do* anything with resentment other than learn to live with it, in the hopes it gets smaller, like a cancer in remission.

All of that resentment had to take a backseat in the final week of Vijay's life, when Ma nursed her to her final breaths. "I just wanted to save her. I just wanted my big sister. I just wanted Vijay."

I thought I believed there were some things too heinous to be forgiven, but now I don't know what to believe. We've experimented with the threshold of the unforgivable across so many generations of our women, in the things done to us and by us.

I wonder if our tolerance for evil is simply too high for this world, as our benchmark for bad things gets pushed further and further back by our own traumas. We are so hardened by so many things that happen to us, lotteries of birth into circumstances we never chose, until all we know is how to take up the mantle of performing that script ourselves.

People often say that you learn from trauma and, with luck, even grow from it. But something's lost every time. I have so many doubts about what we must do with it, where we should put it, and how we should channel it. How do we juggle the contradictions of loving people who hurt us? Even now, I still don't know.

Vijay loved a father who brutalized her within an inch of her life, then spent what little was left of her short life after his death looking for him in every man she thought she loved. Ma grieves to the point of delirium for a sister who never believed her about the worst thing that could happen to a person, and has spent every day since trying to fill shoes of indefinite size. Jeev took Vijay's man, betrayed her trust, but was her closest confidant by her own daughter's description.

What I do know is these women lived and continue to. Perhaps that's the best we can do in the pursuit of better versions of ourselves.

Today I find myself at a crossroads of how I feel about Vijay. I cannot bring myself to forgive her for turning a blind eye to Ma's rape, for victimizing her youngest sister who helplessly aches 22 years after her death. In some way it's a selfish resentment, because I mourn the softer mother I could have known had Vijay done her duty as a big sister. A mother who might have noticed the sexual abuse I was experiencing when I was eight years old too. Then again, would I have a mother to know without her?

It feels fateful that as I write this, Natty has discovered she's pregnant with her second child. I have so many hopes for that child. Natty and her husband have done a fine job with their first, Diyaksha. She just turned 13. She's a smart kid. She has a reserved disposition like I did at that age, but she harbors a world of curiosity and potential waiting to explode on this world. Like all of our women, I hope she gets a chance. I hope her future sibling gets a chance. I hope all of Vijay's grandchildren across her three children have more chances than she did — than all of them did.

I hope that her unborn child knows love. That they never know such pain as the women who came before them, and if they do that they'll be shielded, or comforted. At least believed. Most of all, healed. I hope they know their grandmother, their Athas, and their sisters in arms. They don't need your judgment or sympathy, although you're free to dispense it. What they need is grace, to be seen in their fullest complexity, and to be learned from.

Vijay is a myth, an inspiring and cautionary tale to raise a child on. She was a firecracker, with a red-hot temper and a penchant for brandy. An addict, who gambled her life away on a blackjack table. She was a woman scorned, and a scared child weary of the world. A god too revered to be a woman who was loved. A person whose shortcomings left devastation in their wake, and whose bravery can never be repaid. She is an imperfect and irreplaceable bedrock. She tried, and often failed, but god dammit she tried.

UNFINISHED BUSINESS

Maria Mantas

The road to the cemetery is uphill and narrow. So are most of the streets in Nestani but my father navigates them with ease. He parks next to the church that overlooks the graves and treks down the stairs onto a dirt path. He takes out the bag he keeps in his car and gets to work. He will refill the oil lamps, clear away fallen branches, light candles and make the sign of the cross while saying a greeting to his father.

In death, just as in life, my grandfather receives the unconditional affection of his son.

My grandfather died in August of 2005 from pancreatic cancer. His health had been poor for months. We flew to Greece from the

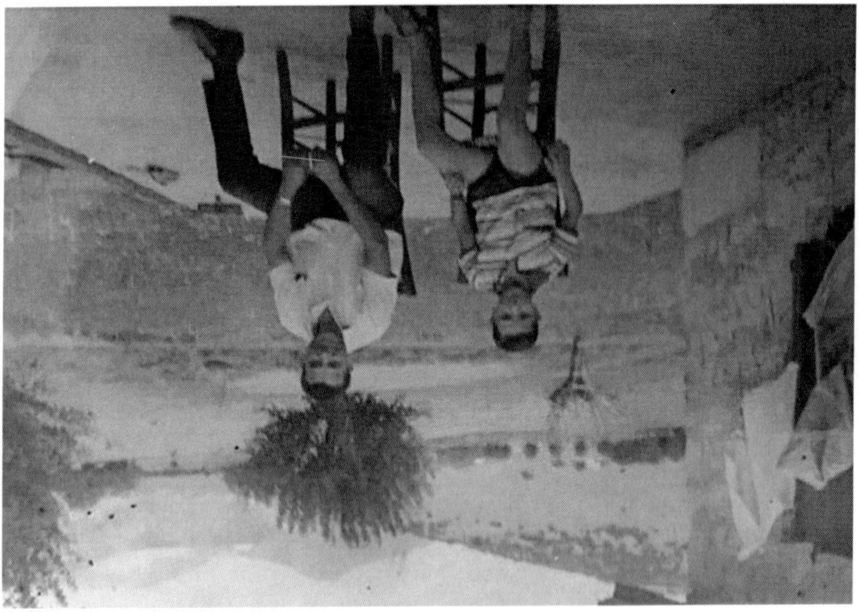

States to be with him. The night before he died my mother saw him in a dream. She knew it was time. "Go to the hospital," she told my father in the morning. My grandfather died that afternoon.

I don't remember him at all. Everything I know about him has been told to me by others: *He was a hothead, but he loved his grandkids. He was particular about the amount of salt in his food. He had a voice that could fill a room.*

Yet the gravity of his presence in my father's life has always been palpable.

"He was my god," my father says. And as it is with gods, sacrifices must sometimes be made.

My father's earliest career aspiration was to become a truck driver. It wasn't because he was particularly interested in trucks or driving around Greece. "I just thought it was a nice job to have because that's what my dad did."

My grandfather was 11 years old when World War II began. His schooling was interrupted, and in a time of poverty across Greece, his family suffered: he sold eggs, made straw brooms, and even sat on the street, begging.

It was only after the war when he enrolled in the army to complete his mandatory service that he found a sense of stability. He didn't have an education beyond elementary school, but he learned how to drive. So that's what he did; upon his discharge he became a truck driver. He spent 20 years moving products along Greece's winding roads.

He could afford to marry my grandmother and they had three children. They lived in a one bedroom house in Nestani by the church that anchored the village. My grandfather would be gone for days at a time – sometimes 10 or 20 – but the family was always fed.

"Nothing," my father said, "was ever missing."

My father, the middle child, was a good student. He excelled at math and after high school he earned admission to a college in the city of Thessaloniki, a six-and-a-half hour drive from Nestani. The city was big and different and he couldn't imagine living so far from his family. So he told my grandfather he changed his mind; he wasn't ready to start college. Instead, he'd sit for the PanHellenic Exams – the qualifying tests to get into college in Greece – again in the summer. Maybe he could study somewhere closer.

In September of 1978 he enrolled for classes at the National and Kapodistrian University of Athens. It was only two hours away from Nestani, and he would be living with his mother's sister. He no longer wished to be a truck driver. He thought he might make a good math teacher.

The following year two students from Nestani asked if he'd want to room with them. He jumped at the chance. He moved out of his aunt's home to an apartment so cramped he had to share a bedroom. But he didn't mind; he was ready to be more independent. He was 19 and living in a neighborhood lined with tavernas and discotheques. And once my father realized which classes didn't *require* attendance, he found time to frequent them all.

He studied geometry, trigonometry, algebra, statistics, even meteorology. His life as an academic was becoming a reality.

But in early spring of 1980 my grandfather came to my father with a proposition. There was a plot of land on the side of the road between the cities of Patras and Corinth. It overlooked the Gulf of Patras where ferries would travel between the Rio and Antirrio piers. A man from Nestani had purchased the land and turned it into a gas station – though it looked more like a shed. He wanted to expand by bringing in investors. My grandfather, now a taxi driver, was interested. His older son, Thanasi, had moved to the United States. Thanasi was living in Chicago, working at diners and having fun instead of going to school or the stable job as they had agreed on. My grandfather needed a reason to bring him back. My father could take care of things at the gas station in the meantime.

"So," he asked my father, "what do you think?"

By his third year of college, my father had his own room in the apartment. It didn't really matter, though, because he now spent most of his nights on the cot in the storage room in the back of the gas station. It was a two-hour drive between Athens and Patras, and my father was working 17-hour shifts. There wasn't much downtime; he would fill customers' tanks, wash their windows, fill their tires. The days went by quickly, at least. Then he'd make the drive back to Athens to attend classes. There was no time for discotheques and tavernas.

Meanwhile, renovations on the station were getting expensive. The founding partner had accrued a lot of debt, and was looking for any chance he could to find the money he owed. Someone needed to keep an eye on him, but my grandfather was busy as a driver. So the responsibility fell to my father.

It was the spring of 1982 when my father decided to drop two classes. If he graduated as planned, he would then be required to enter the army – a whole year away from the business. But if he retained his status as a student, he could put off his mandatory service for a while. It was a temporary solution, he reasoned, and wouldn't be a problem. He could always come back – he *would* come back – to finish his degree. And in the meantime, he'd help his father by keeping an eye on his partner.

I was on spring break when I was admitted to graduate school. I was in a Dollar Tree with my sister. We were putting together Easter baskets for our cousins when I felt the buzz on my watch. I was sure I'd be rejected. I called my father immediately. By the time we arrived home 20 minutes later he had called everyone in the family.

He told me it would be an honor for him just to walk onto the campus. "And now you get to pass through it," he said. "Isn't that amazing?"

My father completed his military service but when he was discharged he did not return to school. By then my uncle Thanasi returned from Chicago and together the brothers managed two of their father's gas stations.

My grandfather never insisted that my father stay in the business. In fact, he lamented until his death that my father never finished his education.

"Yianni only had a few classes left," he often told my mother. "He would've been a teacher now."

My father bears no resentment toward my grandfather. He likes his work, he says. And besides, he still gets to do math, managing the business' finances. I have never heard my father talk of his decision to abandon his studies. He just did it because that, I have come to see, is what he saw as his obligation to his father.

When we visited the campus in May my father took photos of everything. He pointed out the names of Greek philosophers inscribed across the front of the library. He questioned whether I might consider completing a PhD after my Master's.

"There's nothing better," he said, "than being a student, after all."

THE JOURNEY TO ETHAN

Nikaline McCarley

My body felt like a time bomb. It had betrayed me in the cruelest of ways. It was not just the threat of cancer. My body was withholding the possibility of giving birth again. A small part of me never trusted my anatomy. I had grown up in the 1990s and like most young girls I had punished, shamed, and starved myself in all the expected ways. But this latest fuck you from my body was infinitely more difficult to absorb. It broke my heart.

March 21, 2019: New Jersey Turnpike
The drive clocked 45 minutes on Google maps but felt interminable. I shifted in the passenger seat trying to find comfort.

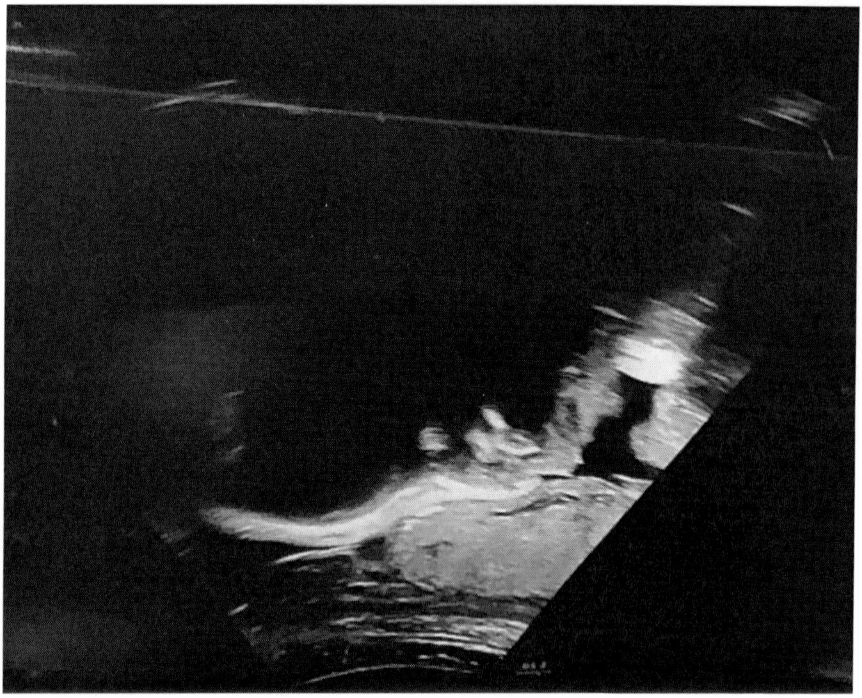

The rental smelled of Clorox wipes. I gripped the worn leather so tightly my knuckles turned white.

I remember that it was raining hard. My husband was driving me to a fertility clinic to implant our embryo into a surrogate so that we might have another child.

The last thing I remember before the doctor called was the blurriness of the windshield as condensation fogged the glass and mirrors. I answered my cell and my husband lowered the volume of the car radio.

"Nikaline? Are you driving?" the doctor asked.

"Yes, we are about 30 minutes away from your office. Is everything ok?"

"I'm going to need you to pull over."

October 2015: New York City

I was lying in bed, 11 weeks pregnant, scrolling through Facebook when it was still relevant. I felt safe under a light blue duvet. I was three months pregnant and my anxiety felt normal, appropriate even. Then my husband Darren said "Alexa has breast cancer. Did you know?"

She is a first cousin on my father's side. We hadn't spoken in months. But Darren had just seen her social media post announcing that she was a BRCA1 carrier and that she had just been diagnosed with breast cancer. At this point I was vaguely aware of the BRCA gene; Angelina Jolie wrote an Op-Ed in *The New York Times* about her own BRCA diagnosis and double mastectomy. I somehow knew that only five percent of the population carried the gene mutation. I did not believe this information pertained to me.

Still, I called my mother for reassurance. She calmly explained that she had no history of breast cancer and reminded me that I recently had blood work and genetic testing done while trying to become pregnant.

Nonetheless I emailed my fertility physician asking if I had been tested for the BRCA1 gene. I assumed that I had and that it was negative because all other blood work had been normal. Besides, Alexa was my father's sister's daughter and I always believed breast cancer was only hereditary if it came from the mother's side of the family. I was wrong. I fell asleep that night not knowing that in the morning my body was going to hijack me.

Early 1900s: Sparta, Greece

My aunt Mary had just returned home from getting a haircut. She was eager to catch up and chat about our family's history, even though we both knew the conversation would be difficult. She was now in her 70s and living in Portland, Oregon. She had also been diagnosed with breast cancer when she was 42 years old.

Mary reminisced about our relatives who came to the United States in 1906 from a small village outside of Sparta in Greece. The first relative to die from breast cancer was my great grandmother Anastasia Chunus. It is believed Anastasia carried a BRCA mutation, although she was never tested.

Anastasia had followed her husband from Sparta to Pocatello, a small rural community in southeast Idaho. There my great grandfather bought land and ran a sheep herding business. She gave birth to nine children and ultimately died young from breast cancer, leaving my great grandfather alone.

"My earliest recollections are the stories from Aunt Dee and my mom about my *yiayia* dying at 50 and leaving nine children for my *papou* to care for," Mary said. "And he literally lost his mind." Of those nine children and their offspring, almost every woman either had BRCA or was diagnosed with breast or ovarian cancer.

This is where I was when I found out I was one of them: I was about to set off on a sunset cruise in Kauai with Darren when I got a call from a geneticist. Haunted by the news about my cousin, I had a blood test for the mutation. I was beginning to feel better as my first trimester was coming to an end. Still, I was nervous about the test. The geneticist, who I recall as remote, nonetheless sounded sad when she told me, "it's positive."

My daughter was born in April and three months later I began six months of screening for breast cancer, alternating between MRIs and mammograms.

Dr. Mark E. Robson, chief of breast services at Memorial

Sloan Kettering, is recognized as a leading BRCA expert. He later told me that "in the 1970s really, cancer was thought to be largely an environmental disease because our understanding of DNA and the applications of DNA were still pretty rudimentary because the technology for sequencing was still slow and expensive." But then a clinician began noticing cancer diagnoses within the same families. That, in turn, ultimately led to the discovery of genetic mutations such as BRCA1 and BRCA2. People who inherit a BRCA mutation have an increased risk of developing certain kinds of cancers, specifically breast and ovarian, over a lifetime.

I had always believed that my positive BRCA test was the result of some incestual sexual consummation of siblings marrying each other in the small Spartan village where my ancestors had once lived.

It was not incestuous. "Somebody in your family's distant, distant past was unfortunate enough to have the mutation develop probably when they were either an early embryo or maybe even just the egg or the sperm," said Robson.

What did this mean for my daughter? She cannot be tested until she is 25. Can the gene mutation somehow just be fixed before then?

"Well," Robson said, "you can't fix the gene because the alteration is present in every cell of the body and right now we don't have the technology to go in and correct, correct is too strong a word, re-engineer the gene in every cell. And we certainly couldn't do it in every cell of the breast."

January 2018: New York City

I had been through a grueling round of IVF, attempting to make an embryo that would not carry the BRCA1 mutation. Through a process called preimplantation genetic diagnosis, or PGD, embryos can be tested for the BRCA gene, thus allowing parents to determine if they want to implant a BRCA affected embryo or not. Through IVF, my husband and I were able to create six embryos, four that were male with the BRCA gene mutation and two that were female and BRCA free. But there was a problem.

During one of my routine scans during IVF, a fertility doctor noticed I had residual scar tissue in the lining of my uterus from the previous birth of my daughter, resulting in what is known as Asherman syndrome.

The birth of my daughter Liv about two years earlier had been a difficult one. During my 40-week ultrasound, we learned that Liv had not gained weight between weeks 37 and 40 and that the placenta had likely stopped working, prohibiting her from receiving the necessary nourishment she needed for survival. I was rushed to the hospital that day to be induced and Liv's birth resulted in an emergency C section.

In the weeks following Liv's delivery, I began hemorrhaging. Another ultrasound found that from giving birth I had developed placenta accreta, a condition which, according to The Cleveland Clinic, "occurs during pregnancy when the placenta attaches too deeply into the wall of your uterus." Another surgery was required to stop the bleeding and remove the residual product of the unwanted placenta. This surgery is what my physicians believe resulted in the formation of scar tissue of my uterus, making it very difficult for me to carry another child. Yet another surgery was recommended to remove the destructive scar tissue.

March 2017: New York City

I was at work at CNN when I took a call from an oncologist at NYU. I was planning a girls' trip to Las Vegas to see Britney Spears and was flying out the next day. I was anxious about the results after a biopsy had detected some suspicious cells in my breast tissue. I kept calling the doctor even though I just wanted to be able to go on my trip.

"You hanging in there?" she asked.

"What are my results? I asked.

She said, "It's DCIS with microinvasion."

"What the hell is that?" I asked.

She explained that my cancer, while mostly limited to the milk duct, was starting to spread.

"Do I have to cancel my trip?" I asked. You do ask the dumbest questions when you're in shock.

I was told that I needed to be admitted immediately and because I carried the BRCA gene, I would have to undergo a double mastectomy to stop the spread. If I waited, I would also have to go through chemotherapy.

March 2018: New York City

I was sitting on the couch in my apartment in lower Manhattan when Dr. Sheeva Talebian called. She is a reproductive endocrinologist and had been my fertility doctor throughout my first pregnancy and had become a physician I trusted implicitly. I remember her asking if I had a second to chat. Calls like these were never good news.

She told me my latest ultrasound scan detected scar tissue on the lining of my uterus and that carrying a baby to term could be challenging. She did, however, recommend that we go ahead and implant the healthiest girl embryo. It was worth a shot. She also warned me that implantation might not succeed given the damaged state of my uterus.

Two weeks later, to everyone's amazement including my own, I was pregnant. But this time I was not filled with elation. I was anxious and afraid.

I miscarried seven weeks later.

January 1st, 2019: New York City via Skype

Darren cleaned our bedroom, fluffing pillows, smoothing out the duvet, picking up clothing from the floor and hanging it in the closet. I felt the need to put on makeup. None of this made sense because the conversation we were about to have would take place over Skype.

The couple we were meeting appeared on the computer screen at exactly 4 o'clock. We began by making small talk. We could all feel the awkwardness of the situation.

We were interviewing one another. We were searching for a surrogate. They were deciding if they wanted to help us.

I asked her whether she had viewed the profiles of other couples. Later, she told me, "You were the first and only."

We were going to be partners in a journey unlike any other. We wanted another child. I could not carry one. She could.

March 21, 2019: Basking Ridge, New Jersey

Our surrogate and her husband had flown into New Jersey to implant our baby. She had gone through her own medical screening a month earlier in New Jersey because surrogacy was then illegal in New York. We transferred our embryos from New York to a fertility clinic to proceed legally. The four of us agreed to meet at a nearby coffee shop.

I stared down at an empty plate. My legs were shaking beneath the table. She and her husband walked in soaked from the rain but excited. I went to the bathroom because I did not want them to see me cry. Darren told them we had gotten a troubling call from the doctor on the way over.

March 21, 2019: New Jersey Turnpike Part II. One hour earlier.

On the phone our fertility doctor told us that the girl embryo – the last BRCA unaffected one that we had – did not survive the thaw. He gave us two options. We could call this off and we could go back to New York, do another round of IVF to try for another BRCA free embryo. Or we could implant a BRCA1 affected boy embryo that day. If we chose the latter, he said, the embryo would need about an hour to thaw to see if it could survive and be viable for implantation. We had five minutes to decide.

He was still on the speaker phone as Darren turned to me defeated but also trying to console. "Look, at this point, this is just a normal Thursday for us," he said. "What do you want to do?"

April 2023: Rye, New York

My son's name is Ethan. He is three years old. He is stubborn, defiant and will not eat anything nutritious. He has the best smile in the world.

He likes dinosaurs and race cars. He and his sister fight a lot. He follows her everywhere. Liv, who is seven, is protective of him but gets jealous when the attention falls on him.

I worry about him all the time. Sometimes when I look at him I think, is this real?

THE REUNION

Langchen Sun

Please be advised that this story includes references to and descriptions of suicide.

In the kitchen, she slowly washed the fish and pulled out their spines. She had already prepared seven dishes. As she was cleaning the fish, the door quietly opened. A man all in black slipped in and cautiously peeked inside. He heard a sound from the kitchen and breathed a long sigh of relief.

It had been two years and seven days since the last time he was home.

If it were not the Chinese traditional New Year, Zang wouldn't be preparing that much more than enough for two people.

Li didn't realize that Zang had breathed a long sigh of relief too,

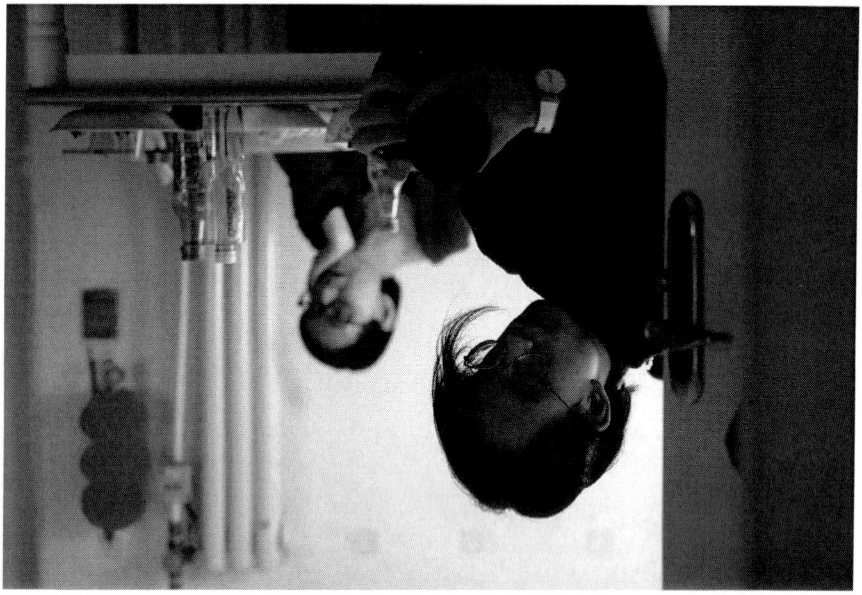

covered by the slight sound Li made when he closed the door.

To Li, the house looked as it always did with a few new red lanterns hanging next to the water pipe. Li quietly walked into the living room, where Zang stepped outside the kitchen too. Their eyes met.

"Hi," Li said to his mother.

"You're back," she replied. Her face betrayed nothing.

The so-called family photo was taken on this day.

As a student who has been learning cinematography and movie making at the University of London Art for three years, Li has dealt with countless photos and movies that involved sensational moments around human relationships, but none of them were about himself or his family. This was the first one.

Usually, a family photo is taken with people lining up, all facing straight at the camera, with big smiles on their faces. But here you can see the difference. Li told me about the moment he took the photo: He sat in front of the mirror, held the camera, and left himself in the dark side. His mother sat behind. She was meant to be the main subject but turned out to be out of focus. Li told me this was the way he found it "comfortable" to take a family photo. He thought his mother had been aware of having her photo taken, but she just "doesn't care."

In the two years and seven days he was away from home, Li says he thought of his family many times, but he seldom had the desire to return home. "It's because of the pandemic," he says. "But from my inner heart, I know it's not." He sometimes felt afraid to face his parents, but in another way, he also felt uncomfortable that he was always on his own. "We only Facetime when we think we need to," he says. "But there's seldom a time when we both feel there's a necessity."

In China, most of the "Z generation"—those born after 2000—grew up in a rather protective environment. This includes abundant material support and a high educational demand in childhood. This also involves a more restrictive and limited environment for children's choices.

In the meantime, especially in big cities, children in the Z generation are expected to excel at every skill. Therefore, parents spend as much time and care as possible to ensure their children grow up well, what we call "tough love." In what is seen as a typical upper middle-class Asian family, most of us indeed are expected to be a lawyer, a doctor, or a teacher. It's abnormal if you study the arts or make it a career.

Li never experienced anything like that. When he was four years old, he first showed interest in movies. He accidentally found a camera in his grandfather's grocery box, and with no guidance, he became captivated by the image in the aperture. His parents didn't spend much time with him while he was in kindergarten and primary school, and the camera was his only friend.

Normally, when a child witnesses classmates whose parents surround them, they might feel lonely. But that was not Li. He felt a sense of freedom even at a young age. Looking back, though, he feels differently about that bleak period. "It was after I grew older," he says, "when I found I wanted to have parents participating in my life."

The reason his parents did not was simple: By the time Li was nine, his father had lung cancer, and a year later his parents got divorced. His father survived but left the family and him.

That was also the time when Li's idea of building a career in making movies sprouted. He wanted to be a director. His mother expressed no worry about that.

"I can't tell if that's an excuse for irresponsibility or if she wants to give me freedom and grow up naturally," Li says. He always remembered that his mother told him about giving him much more freedom than other parents of our generation.

Li later concluded this lack of attention from his parents came from the absence of feeling like a family. "It definitely gives me space," he says, "but I'm also isolated." Li has complex feelings about these relationships.

Li remembers when he and his parents traveled to Hong Kong. He was nine and they were all together wandering on a street. It was only at that moment that felt he had a family. But there was also a feeling he would not have the family soon.

Li's mother Zang was born in a small city in the northeastern province of Heilongjiang in 1973. She had three older brothers and an older sister. Her parents were accountants who struggled to earn enough money to pay for all their children to have college educations. Even so, Zang thinks of her parents as "intellectuals".

Youngsters back then were seen as "the generation of revolution". They were born just on the edge of the Cultural Revolution of the late 1960s and early 1970s, and no one had a clear idea of what the future would be. Society had yet to fully recover from the chaos, death, and terror of those years. People didn't know what they should do, or be. People were poor and there was little time for worrying about parents and children communicating.

"I never talked to my parents about anything," Zang says. She thought it was a normal situation. She wrote, and that was her only escape. "Over time I got used to saying nothing to them," Zang told me.

It's hard to know whether Zang shared values, thoughts, or emotions with her parents. There was no room for feelings. The agricultural society they had come from left the reinforcement that parents should have more than one child. But in the cities that was difficult. Still, Zang didn't seem to hold a grudge against her parents. And she had bigger ambitions.

She excelled at math in school. She was always recognized as the smartest student in the class. But she failed to get a high enough grade on her university entrance exam to qualify for the top schools. So instead she chose a lower-tier school. College life was far from what she wanted. Still, she was determined to attend graduate school in Beijing afterward.

While Zang told me the story without emotion, Li told it differently. In his memory, his mother told him about her preparation for the postgraduate examination several times, and it became the most memorable part of her story. "Nosebleed while reading in the hallway" was a phrase that he mentioned several times when he recalled their conversations.

By that time in China, an undergraduate degree was enough to secure a good job. As the youngest child, Zang did not have to worry about supporting her family. She was free to go to graduate school.

She was admitted to a better university in Beijing, and that year she wrote about her life.

"When I got rid of a familiar and unchanging life as I wanted, I found that I had nothing left. I found a wider sky, but under the sky, I couldn't find the familiar pair of wings. At the price of loneliness, I can't tell what I'm looking for after all. I just don't want to stand on the horizon of age 25 and see through the scenery of age 52 at a glance. This is the reason for my existence."

That same year she met and fell in love with Li's father. She called this "the start of another world".

Li didn't come home to see his mother. It was because of a broken heart after his breakup with his girlfriend. "I have nowhere to go but home," Li told me.

Though he didn't tell his mother about his girlfriend, he did tell her that he was coming to visit. His mother didn't ask why. But in a subtle way, she asked him to come sooner.

Since Li's childhood, he says, he and his mother have been able to talk about everything. He says he felt no burden talking with his mother, and he knows she understands him. Still, he seldom starts a conversation with her. His mother usually initiates the talk. But this time she didn't. Zang sensed that Li was having a difficult time and by now was reluctant to ask any questions.

Even before Li decided to study abroad, he had discussed with his mother whether she needed him to be at home. His mother wanted to respect his choice. They seem to share the same thought: they don't want to influence each other on their own paths.

After Li flew to England for school, some of Zang's relatives talked behind his back, thinking Li should have stayed with his mother who was lonely. Li missed his mother sometimes, but the only time she asked him to come home was when the relatives began saying things. But Li did not come home. He chose his wishes over his mother's.

That was also the first time he attempted suicide. It is something he does wish to talk about. He has never told his mother. Instead, he speaks about suicide through his work. He made a film about a young artist's career and emotional struggles. Li's movie earned praise and was a finalist in a film competition in England. Li feels this success came at a time when he was at his lowest. The artist in his movie reflected this; he used blood to paint at the end of the story.

The success of the movie also coincided with Li's decision to reject his mother's request that he come home. He says he feels deep regret about this. He had never thought about making a film about his mother and family. But he has changed his mind. He's embarking on a project about them and is still deciding where to produce it. He will be graduating soon and is unsure whether to stay in London or return to China. He says he feels a kind of "emotional connection" to home and has started to think about what a family is.

After life began for Zang's "another world", things went well at first.

"We share the same interest in math, we came from the same place, and he treated me well." Zang sighed as she told me about the relationship between her and Li's father.

This was not to last. Reality is never going to let you meet the happy ending like the fairytale.

She blames her former husband's family and growing up.

"My parents are all intellectuals, but his parents are businessmen," she says. "I didn't see anything wrong here but found out I was wrong. There's a huge difference between us."

The burden of being a wife and mother, as well as a mathematician, was more than she had expected.

"By the time I had Li, I was 27, no one was even that certain about themselves at 27," Zang says. "We were all still in the mood of happiness, and Li's father had no thought about what was ahead."

This was the second time she had described her life and future as "uncertain." It is also the last time she spoke to me about her parents.

After Li was born, Zang always asked his father to spend more time with him. Instead, she says, he played computer games after work. Li's father thought he had already taken on so much responsibility just by providing financial support.

"If only I knew things would turn out to be like that, I wouldn't have forced him," Zang says. In 2009, after a "cold war" between the couple, Li's father found out that he had lung cancer. His parents and sister came to Beijing to take care of him. They all lived together.

This was when the nightmare for Zang began. Li's father's sister and mother kept criticizing Zang for being an irresponsible wife to her face. It all became too much. They divorced a year later after Li's father had recovered. Within a few months, he met another woman and started a new family. Zang was devastated.

"It's a time I can't even deal with myself," Zang says. "I was choking. I couldn't get to the shore." Both she and Li's father couldn't make it to Li at the time.

Li has no memory or feelings about what was taking place around him. He was off by himself. When his father left his mother told him he had gone on "a long trip".

"I was protecting him," Zang says.

But, says Li, "I was losing part of myself."

Zang knew that her son was sensitive but regrets not telling him the truth. "I hesitated several times if I should tell him the whole story now. It's just I don't feel used to doing that."

She had lost the desire to write. Once again she kept her feelings to herself.

Li can remember everything that took place on his visit home for the Chinese New Year.

After he and his mother greeted each other with "Hi", they were in awkward silence. They sat on the sofa, watched television, and did not speak.

"Peng!" The silence was broken when they heard fireworks exploding outside their window.

"Instead of looking at the glamorous fireworks," Li says, "she looked back," Li remembers being surprised as his mother stared straight at his face.

"When the fireworks lit up his face, I was surprised too," Zang says. She paused. "Surprised that he's grown up."

At that moment she felt a strong desire to tell her son about everything.

They looked at each other for a few seconds, which felt like a century.

Zang quietly stood up and returned to the kitchen.

Li says, "That's the moment when I realized, I should take a photo of her, or, of us."

He followed his mother quietly into the kitchen. The ice didn't break in a second; it had been too long for that. But they felt it.

Li later left a post on Instagram post after that day.

"Chinese New Year. Does my mom look like me?

It's been 5 years since I spent time of the Chinese New Year with family members. I nearly forgot how it feels like. In other words, I've not been celebrating new year or Christmas properly for 5 years. I forgot how everything stops during holiday seasons, and how it allows you to have a moment of dizziness, a dizziness where you are allowed to feel out of life, out of something that's complicated and confusing, and just go with the moment. I haven't had that moment for so long.

I never known why people have holidays. Now I know, this is one of the most special Chinese New Year for me. I really almost forgot that I somehow had a family."

There he left the photo with these words.

There was their reunion.

WHERE HOPING GETS YOU

Emma Rose

Please be advised that this story includes references to and descriptions of suicide.

A text from Mom broke my stride. I was walking along the East River when her first text landed, followed by another and another.

She had been going through her father's belongings that had been sitting in the basement of her parents' house. Her father had died fifteen years earlier and now she needed to tell what she was finding. His birth certificate. His father's death certificate. Documents and papers, but only one photograph.

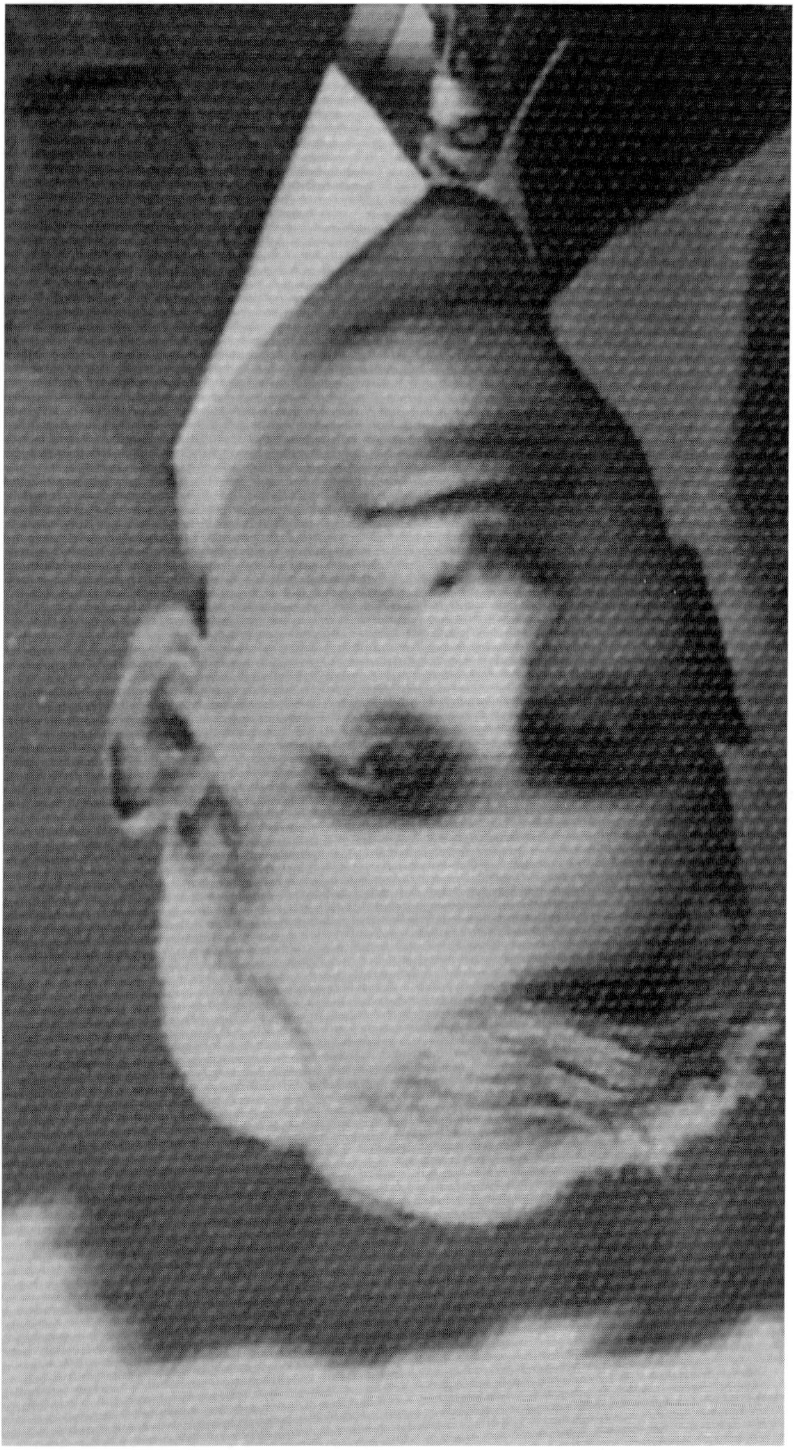

"A picture of Morris and Jennie together!" she texted.

Morris Gollobin and Jennie Levine Gollobin – my grandfather Leonard's parents, her grandparents, my great-grandparents – circa 1925. A black-and-white photograph of a young woman with done-up hair next to a dapper man in a dark suit.

She was excited to find it. I was excited to see it. I had only seen photos of Jennie in her later years. And now we could both finally see what Morris looked like. He died in 1930, when Leonard was only a year old.

"I can't believe he was blonde!!" I wrote back to my mom.

"Or gray." she countered. After all, he would have been almost 50 in the photograph.

"True," I said. "But I'd like to think it's blonde."

We didn't know a lot about Morris and what we did know was not good. People barely talked about him and when they did they told how he had abandoned his wife and infant son. That he had a second family. That he had taken his own life.

I bore barely any resemblance to the relatives on my mother's side of the family. Yet the man in the photograph looked like me. I immediately cropped the image of Morris and saved it to my phone.

I hoped that the photograph my mother sent me was a missing link to my family and its enduring mystery. So I set out to find Morris, to find the ghost in the photograph.

Perhaps I might even be the one to redeem him.

All I had to start were a few sketchy details. Morris lived in New York City at the turn of the 20th century. He was an immigrant from Russia. He must have spoken Yiddish because my great-grandmother, Jennie, barely spoke any English. Jennie was a bitter woman who never — ever — spoke of Morris.

He left a trail of public records: Morris Gollobin (alternatively Maris Gollobin, Morris Gollabin, Morris Galuben, Morris Galenben) was born in either September 1875 or 1877 in Russia. He immigrated in October of 1891 to New York City. Nine years later, the census taker still listed his immigration status as "alien."

In 1900, he was 25 and boarding in the home of Samuel and

Rebecca Ginsberg at 77 Market Street in Manhattan. His marital status was single, and his occupation was listed as "druggist." He could read, write and speak English.

Five years later he was listed as the head of a household and living at 1908 Bergen St. in Brooklyn. He had a wife, Augusta. They had married in Manhattan on March 20, 1904. They had a four-month-old son, Sidney. Living with them was his brother-in-law, Samuel Weinstein, and an 18-year-old Austrian servant named Etta Stecker. Augusta and Samuel had both immigrated to the United States from Russia.

By 1910, the Gollobins were living at 277 South Fourth St. in Williamsburg. Morris was now a naturalized American citizen. They had a new servant, 22-year-old Mary Grabovisky from Poland. Morris rented the apartment and was listed as the proprietor of a drug store. Augusta also spoke, read and wrote English.

The family moved again. In 1915, they moved to 1783 Bedford Ave., a block from Prospect Park. They had a second child, an infant son, Arthur. Sidney was now 10 and attended school. Morris was still a pharmacist. Augusta and Morris ran the drug store together. Their new servant, 23-year-old Eva Cater, was a Russian immigrant.

The family was back in Manhattan five years later, renting an apartment at 180 Edgecombe Ave., in Hamilton Heights, just across the Harlem River from Yankee Stadium. They had taken in a boarder, a 23-year-old Russian man.

And that was where the record ended. Morris and Augusta worked together, had two sons, could afford servants, though they did take in a boarder. Augusta was registered as a Manhattan voter as late as 1924. She listed her address as 133 West 120th St. Morris's name was notably absent from the rolls.

In 1928, Augusta's name popped up in a Hackensack, N.J. city directory for The Knitwear Shoppe. Sidney was listed as the store's salesman.

In 1930, Augusta, now 50, appeared in the census as the widowed head of her household in Hackensack, living alone and working as the proprietor of her knitwear store.

By then, however, Morris had already met Jennie. They had had a child, my grandfather.

And Morris was dead.

I wanted to know whether Morris had left a mark. Was he connected to his community as so many Eastern European immigrants were? Was he involved with a synagogue? Was he more than just a pharmacist?

It turns out he was. In 1906, he sat on the committee for a charity event at a local Jewish orphanage, the Brooklyn Hebrew Orphan Asylum. Augusta was a member of the Jewish ladies' society. Sidney, meanwhile, was a star athlete in high school, breaking track and field records. His name appeared in the newspaper.

But Morris had not come alone to America. He was the eldest of five brothers — Jacob, David, Harry and Israel. They also had two sisters, Annie and Sarah. They had come with their father, Isaac. They also had a stepmother, Chave, the mother of the two youngest children. A year after their arrival, however, Isaac died and the family was so poor that three weeks after his death Chave surrendered her three youngest children to the Hebrew Orphan Asylum in Brooklyn.

The admission roll listed the boys as Harry, 10; David, 8; and Israel, 6. That would be the last public record of Chave Gollobin.

Years later, Morris played a role in the effort to bring music to the orphanage. Still, it is unknown whether he ever visited his siblings at the orphanage.

When I was younger and curious about hereditary illness, I asked my parents: who in our family had gotten sick? What have people died from? Are any of these ailments genetic? Are there any I should be getting routinely tested for?

Their answers were comforting. We are a physically healthy family. Many of the women in my family have lived into their 90s. Nothing that I should be concerned about. Or so I thought.

The Gollobin family history is a story of a precarious and harrowing medical history that no DNA ancestry test could have ever told. It had been kept a family secret for nearly a century.

It does not end with Morris. Among the papers my mother had

found was his death certificate. The report reads: "The chief or determining cause of his death was: hydrocyanic poisoning, suicide."

As a druggist, he likely had easy access to cyanide.

So the rumors were true: a suicide.

I then found the death certificates of his siblings – David, Harry, Jacob, Israel and Annie. Sarah's was the only one missing.

Jacob's death certificate listed the cause as "hydrocyanic acid poisoning." His suicide by ingesting cyanide was on September 11, 1914 at the age of about 34 – 16 years before Morris met the same fate.

Then there was David. He died on February 3, 1934, four years after Morris, and 20 years after Jacob. His cause of death was listed as "Asphyxiation by Hanging Suicidal."

Next I found Harry, who died on April 26, 1935 of "Suicidal asphyxia."

Then I came to Annie, who was 90 at the time of her death.

I noticed something odd as I inspected her death certificate. She was a patient in a hospital at the time of her death, which at first I didn't find strange. But it wasn't any hospital — it was the Kings Park State Hospital for the Insane. So I looked back at the census records. Annie was listed as a patient (or "insane patient" or "inmate") as early as 1915, when she was 42 years old.

Morris's older sister Annie had spent over half of her life in a psychiatric hospital.

And finally, there was Israel. He was nine when he died. He died from meningitis. He never left the orphanage.

Jennie was named the Administrator of Morris's estate. Not Augusta. But when and how did they meet? Had he already left his family? And what had he left her that was so important that he made her his administrator?

On Leonard's birth certificate, Morris listed his address as 1839 Broadway in Brooklyn. I headed to the Brooklyn Surrogate Courthouse and made my way to the basement and into the records room. The records room is a massive open space with rows and rows of file cabinets labeled by last name. I asked a clerk where I could find records from the 1930s. He looked at me, then looked past me at the thousands of files behind me, then back at me.

"You're going to have to find the card before I can help you," he said.

I found the G's. I thumbed through the Go's. Dozens of them.

Goldman. Goldstein. I found every Jewish "Go-" surname in the book. Except Gollobin.

Maybe the answer was in Manhattan. Morris's last known address on his death certificate was an apartment in Harlem.

Manhattan's record keeping is only slightly more technologically advanced than Brooklyn's. They have a computer from about 1999 with folders labeled "Letters to Will," and "Letters to Administration." I was instructed to search under the former.

Nothing. Damn.

I opened all of the other folders on the desktop. They're organized by the first letter of the last name and then by year.

And under Letters to Administration, I found him: Gollobin Morris 1231 1930 394 149

"I got him!" I said out loud.

"Oh yeah?" said a court officer behind me.

The excitement didn't last.

I stood up to ask the woman behind the desk what to do next.

"Where'd you find it? Under Wills or Administration?" she asked, her voice prickly.

"Administration," I told her.

"Yeah, so he died intestate. There's basically going to be nothing in the file."

I was confused. "Intestate?" I asked.

"Yeah. He died *without a will.*" She put some sour emphasis on that last part.

I explained to her that I had a letter from his attorney to my great-grandmother naming her the…

"…administrator?" She finished my sentence for me.

"Yes," I said.

"Yeah. He died intestate. That letter might be the only thing in the file."

I had hoped that if he indeed started a new family, Morris, whom

WHERE HOPING GETS YOU   71

I assumed was a successful pharmacist, had had the foresight to leave everything to Jennie and my grandfather. But it makes a lot more sense that he would have died by suicide without prior estate planning. I understood that's why my grandfather grew up penniless.

I filled out the form to pull his file. The clerk told me it would take about three weeks for her to get it to me. I think she could sense my disappointment; she then gave me my next lead: if I wanted to get more information on his properties and businesses, try the Department of Finance on John St. It was only a ten-minute walk away. I headed back out into the cold. The records from all five boroughs dating back before the 1960s are housed in a facility in Queens.

I spent four hours combing through old property ledgers. The records are so old they crumble in your hands. When I got home, I noticed my scarf was dotted with little brown scraps.

The records are divided by borough. They are then sorted by block and lot number. I found addresses associated with Morris at various points in his life. I knew he had rented most of the apartments he had lived in, so I didn't expect those addresses to have any record of him. But I also thought he owned properties, given that he ran several drug stores over his life and had also leased units to others. I assumed he was a landlord.

Of the two dozen properties, it turns out he did not own a single one.

He leased a unit in April 1902 at 76 Avenue B in Manhattan and again in April 1905 from Empire Real Estate Company. The company leased the property to another man in February 1906.

On April 25, 1914, he leased space from Mary Hildebrand at 349 Bedford Ave., Brooklyn — the same address Annie Gollobin listed as her permanent residence in the 1915 census while she was institutionalized at the Kings Park State Hospital.

Morris rented the same space on Bedford Avenue from Rosie Schatz on August 31, 1917. On December 9, 1919, he renewed the lease with Rosie and re-leased it to Julius Kerr on the same day. By March 1922, he was no longer associated with the property.

Then in April 1922, he appeared to have leased the corner property at 5117 Fifth Avenue in Brooklyn from John and Mary McGowan.

Two months later he leased it to Herman Mendlowitz. On February 1, 1928, Morris leased the same property to Simeon Goodelman, who leased it to a drug company the same day.

Morris never owned. He was a renter all his life, which meant no property as a legacy to his wife – or wives – and children.

I started to call relatives. I reached out on Facebook to a woman named Sydney, who is also Morris's great-grandchild. I explained we might be related. She already knew we were. She, in turn, told her father, Glenn, about me. He wanted to talk with my mother. Glenn was the child of Sidney, Morris's oldest son from his marriage to Augusta.

He told my mom that Morris was addicted to bromides. Bromides were sedatives used at the turn of the century to cure headaches. Doctors stopped prescribing them by the 1940s because they realized they were, in fact, highly addictive sleeping pills.

Morris, he told her, filed for bankruptcy in the 1920s. In 1922 Morris's fortunes had sunk so low that he was selling his inventory for pennies on the dollar. Sidney had to drop out of Harvard in 1924, after completing just two years at the university. My mom found a record of Sidney, still a star athlete, competing in a track meet in 1922, during his freshman year.

Sidney was bitter toward his father for having to drop out of Harvard. He was listed as a 24-year-old junior at New York Law School in 1929. Only Augusta was listed as his guardian on the form. Glenn said Sidney never spoke of Jennie and Leonard, though he knew they existed. Glenn said his father was fiercely loyal to his mother Augusta, caring for her after she had a stroke in the 1960s.

But Glenn also told my mom that he called Leonard in the 1990s. The call wasn't a surprise to either of them. Both apparently knew the other existed. But Leonard never told anyone about the call.

So Leonard wasn't interested in connecting with his father's family. Maybe this was out of respect for his mother. Jennie had kept Leonard away from Morris's family after completing her role as the administrator of his empty estate.

But most importantly, Glenn told my mom that Morris and Augusta had separated before he met Jennie. He knew nothing about how they met, or anything about their relationship – except for this: Morris was bankrupt and an addict before he met Jennie. And that part of Morris and Augusta's split had to do with what he called "sexual incompatibility." He did not elaborate.

Although she's listed as Morris's widow, there is no evidence that Morris and Jennie ever married. I scrolled through many rolls of microfilm to make sure. But Morris's lawyer, the court and everyone in Morris's family seemed on board with the lie. Not that there was going to be a struggle over assets: Morris died penniless with a business described as "hopelessly insolvent."

Still, they were living as a family when Morris died, as I had always hoped they were.

Meanwhile, I sent Sydney the photograph my mother had sent me. I asked if she recognized the dapper man in the dark suit.

She did not.

This was not who I hoped it would be. This was not Morris. It was not Jennie.

It is a photograph of Jennie's older sister Chaya. Jennie had been one of the few in her family to come to America. Chaya had stayed behind in Luninets – in what is now Belarus. As to the man in the photo? No one knows.

The Nazis killed Chaya. Some 3,000 Jews lived in Luninets when in 1942 the Nazis killed all of the men except for a few tailors and other professionals, murdered all of the women and children a month later, and then killed the remaining few in October. They were rounded into ghettos but never transported to camps, except for the few who went to labor camps.

The Jews of Luninets, including Chaya and her two daughters, Bella and Braindel, were shot dead in their own hometown. I imagine her husband, who I assume is the dapper man in the dark suit, met the same fate.

When I asked my mom why, in the absence of any real evidence, she had told me two years earlier that the man in the photograph was Morris, she laughed.

"I guess I'd hoped that it was."

GIVING THE BIRDS A FACE

Jiayu Liang

Jim Verhagen is standing on a beach, surrounded by naked people. He is fully clothed and looking for a bird.

She is a piping plover named Tacey, and Jim knew he would recognize her when he saw green and yellow bands on the left leg, and red and white bands around the other. He knew this because he had photographed the moment she received her bands three years ago. Now he has brought a 600mm camera lens to a nude beach so he can photograph Tacey once more.

Jim is overdressed for the occasion—not only because he is wearing clothes at all, but also because he is dressed for March when it is June. In his enthusiasm to go find Tacey, he forgot to check the forecast.

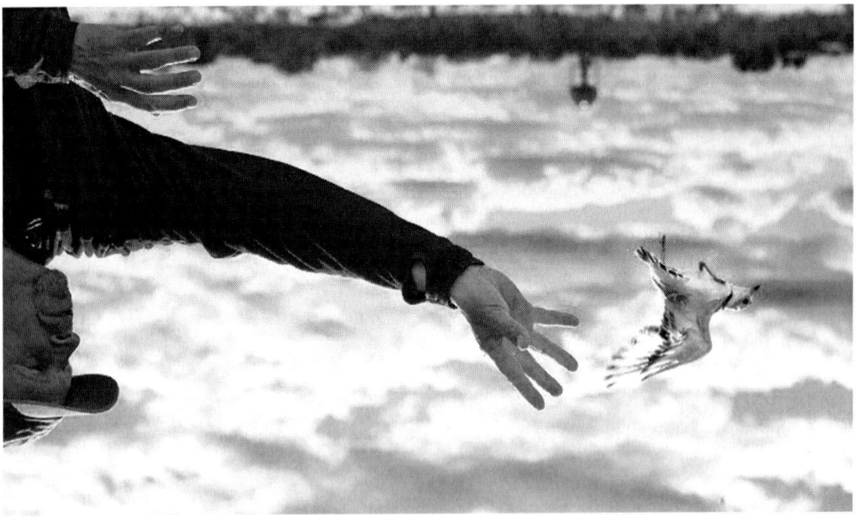

Jim actually knew Tacey's mate, Tufters, first. Both birds and Jim live on Long Beach Island, New Jersey, where Jim grew up and believed for a long time that birds were boring.

Jim is 50 now and wears glasses. He programmed and designed NestStory, an app for biologists to collect and manage data on nesting birds. He came of age surrounded by fishermen and beachgoers who viewed piping plovers as "public enemy number one." They hated that the beaches were shut down to allow the birds to safely breed and hatch.

He likes to joke that on one side of the island, old-timers will tell you that the piping plovers are actually gone. They insist that scientists are hiding the fact that the bird is already extinct so that they can close down the beaches and have it to themselves. On the other side of the island, another group of old-timers will tell you that piping plovers are everywhere – that they saw a hundred of them just yesterday, and the birds aren't endangered at all. They also say scientists are hiding the truth so they can close down the beaches and have it to themselves.

Jim's dad was a nature lover, so Jim grew up with an appreciation for animals even if it didn't necessarily include birds. They spent time on the beaches of the Jersey Shore, something Jim would keep doing with his own daughter. Eventually, Jim would start a blog called "Readings from the Northside" to continue sharing information about the water conditions with his dad after he moved to Virginia.

People on Long Beach Island started following the blog too, to keep up with what was happening in their neighborhood. Jim's audience slowly grew, especially when Hurricane Irene struck in 2011 and people who had evacuated wanted to know how the beach was doing. He borrowed his wife's camera and started taking photos of the beach to accompany the posts. Mostly, he wrote about the water temperatures.

All of that changed with Mac Daddy.

As Jim, his wife, and daughter spent time on the beach they noticed a herring gull that, in Jim's words, looked like crap. He had scraggly feathers and bloodshot eyes, as if every night was a rough night for him. Whenever Jim's family saw a ratty seagull on their

GIVING THE BIRDS A FACE 77

beach trips, they liked to call it Mac Daddy. Eventually it occurred to them that maybe they were seeing the same gull every time.

They noticed how this particular gull foraged differently from other birds; he sat on the edge of the beach, watching and waiting for beachgoers to leave their towels and go into the water. Jim documented Mac Daddy's exploits with his camera.

All of a sudden, the beach was more than a backdrop and the gulls were more than background characters. They were individuals who lived in the neighborhood, just like Jim, and became local celebrities to him. Mac Daddy knew which foods were easier to grab. Doritos in an open bag were great. Cheez-Its in a box were challenging. A decade later, Jim still laughs when he tells these stories.

One day, Jim says, Mac Daddy showed up looking "particularly crappy." Jim photographed the gull as he went through the usual routine of running over towels and tearing into paper bags to pull out food, when he noticed a young herring gull following Mac Daddy around. He was in disbelief at first that this could be Mac Daddy's baby. But he watched as the youngster followed Mac Daddy everywhere, even pecking at the red spot that would make Mac Daddy vomit food into his mouth.

Jim realized she was Mac Mommy all along.

As Jim started paying more attention to the birds on the beach, he began posting more and more photos of them to his blog. Much of his original audience, which had come for information about beach conditions, was put off by this new content. But Jim didn't care.

Even Jim's own sister left a comment complaining. *Jim, I think you're overdoing it with the birds.*

None of this mattered. Jim was on a trajectory of fascination that was ready to take flight. He started writing more about wildlife. One day Ben Wurst from the Conserve Wildlife Foundation of New Jersey found his blog and invited Jim to an osprey banding.

Jim had seen ospreys from a distance before, but it had never occurred to him that you could go right up to their nest – as long as you're with a licensed bander, of course. Jim called it the "best day of his life."

As he watched Ben put silver bands on the ospreys, Jim realized that the writing on the metal was so small that, even with a telephoto camera lens, he would never be able to read the bands again unless the bird was found dead or injured. Jim wished the bands were more distinctive, so that the next time he saw an osprey at the beach, he could recognize it. He wanted to know who the birds were and asked whether they could put a big letter or bright color on the bands. Ben replied that it was possible, but that they didn't have enough money for individualized bands.

Jim thought this was ridiculous. After all, how much could a little metal band cost? He told Ben he would write a check on the spot.

That was the start of Project RedBand, which gives young ospreys nesting in New Jersey's Barnegat Bay an extra red band. In the winter, the ospreys fly to Central and South America, and now Jim can tell when they come back. The project also gets the public excited about watching the birds and reporting any sightings, which helps scientists collect valuable data.

Ben then connected Jim with his boss Kathy Clark, who asked Jim if there was anything else they could do for him. Jim told her yes, he'd always wanted to see a piping plover in the wild. Kathy responded that she knew just the guy, and that she would introduce him to Todd Pover.

A week later Kathy emailed Jim an apology. Todd said the piping plovers were having a horrible season, and the last thing they needed was a photographer creeping around making things worse. Absolutely not.

That was Jim's first impression of Todd Pover. What a dick, Jim remembers, followed by a quick laugh. No, even though he was heartbroken at the time, he understood and sympathized with Todd's concern. It was a complicated feeling for him to express, but most of all it was disappointment.

A month later, Todd wrote to Jim out of the blue and said that only one pair had survived that season. They abandoned the nest and marched their chicks two miles down the beach and were now running around a crowd of people. Todd figured the birds couldn't be any less hidden, so he might as well tell Jim that they were at Barnegat Lighthouse State Park. If anything, it'd be good to have a friend on the beach keeping an eye on them.

Jim lived three miles from the beach. He dropped everything and headed right over. His feet had barely touched the sand when a piping plover chick ran right past him.

"And the rest is history," he would later say. "My life changed."

What turned out to be three piping plover chicks bewitched Jim, body and soul. Jim's daughter led the naming process, as she had done for all the other birds that had captured her father's imagination: Fluffy, Puffy, and Tufters.

Jim said, "She loves the odd man out trope. She's a storyteller."

The next year, Jim returned to the beach and saw just one plover at the same spot. Plovers tend to return to the same site every year, so he believed it was one of the three original chicks. He decided it was Tufters.

This time around he noticed a discoloration on Tufter's knee. So when Tufters returned the following year with a mate, Jim knew it was him again. His daughter named the mate Tacey.

All the while, Jim was getting to know Todd and other bird scientists. He loved to photograph the moment they banded and released endangered species.

It's a terrible thing to be interested in, Jim says. Scientists hate to be photographed, so they're always frowning. Jim says they also made it seem like he was either in the way or slowing them down. But he insists on staying and has learned to work quickly and get good photos without being too intrusive. It's turned into a little game for him. The scientists always tell him that he shouldn't be there and that they don't want a photo. But once it's done, they always come back and want to see the picture. Nonsense, he says now, you're going to want a photo so I'm going to stay.

Jim says Todd is one of the worst. His natural smile is barely a smile, and when he's forced it looks even worse.

Still, Jim understands where the scientists are coming from. Bandings and releases are serious, time-sensitive, and require a lot of concentration. He says having a wild bird in your hand is a moment of great happiness, but there's also a sadness because you know that you're disrupting the natural order of things.

80 GIVING THE BIRDS A FACE

Ultimately, Jim knows these photos are important and that someday the scientists will appreciate them. He says now he often goes to bandings and releases where he has more experience than the biologists. Jim sometimes even coaches them through how the release goes, like when they try to release the bird while it is facing their body. Jim explains that this doesn't work because the bird doesn't know where to go, so they have to make sure the bird is facing out. It's less stressful for the bird and makes for a better photo.

One of Jim's scientist friends, Michelle Stantial, began a three-year study on piping plover chick mortality at the State University of New York College of Environmental Science and Forestry. It feels symbolic that Tufters and Tacey were the first to be banded. Todd released Tacey, and that's the photo at the start of this story. Jim says it was by far the best photo he had ever taken of Todd, so it felt extra special.

Todd agrees it's a good photo, but has mixed feelings about it. He doesn't like that it shows the hands-on element of working with plovers. He says you need to be careful about the message you send when you show scientists handling birds. The photo doesn't capture the full context of how that moment came to be; they were doing a research project and had to secure permits. Todd himself had been doing this work for 20 years before he handled a bird for the first time.

That was the day Tufters got his bands too. Green and yellow on one leg, red and orange on the other. Jim's camera helps him spot the bands and study the birds, looking more closely and documenting each bird's unique traits for others to see.

Through the years, Jim continued to photograph and blog about Tufters and Tacey. He calls Tufters the most handsome piping plover on the planet and shares his band colors, asking readers to let him know if they see Tufters.

One year, the crows at Barnegat Lighthouse State Park found Tufters and Tacey's nest. It was inside an exclosure, a large cage built to keep predators out, but the crows discovered they could perch on top. There, they would wait for the eggs to hatch and swoop in to eat the chicks as soon as they left the exclosure. Jim knew Tufters and Tacey's eggs would hatch soon and tried to keep the crows away –

mostly by throwing rocks and other objects at them.

As it got later, Jim began to wonder what he was still doing there. Maybe it was time to let nature take its course, he thought. Jim tried to reason that he couldn't save everybody, but even as he left for work he had the grim sense that he was sentencing the chicks to death.

The next morning he came back and found out he was right. All the chicks were dead, and Tufters and Tacey were running around in a panic. Tufters was scraping at the ground to make a new nest and signal that he wanted to start over, but Tacey wasn't interested. As he chased her, they both vanished from Jim's sight.

Later on, another plover tracker spotted Tacey down south, so Jim knew that she survived. But he never saw Tufters again. Maybe he died of an injury, or stress.

"I killed Tufters," Jim said.

By building exclosures to try and protect the plovers, Jim said, they turned the chicks into sitting ducks. The crows learned to recognize the exclosures, and it was all too easy for them to wait on top for the chicks to hatch.

Now, Jim holds crow vigils in honor of Tufters. If he notices that crows have discovered an exclosure, he organizes a group of volunteers to babysit for the first 12 hours as the eggs hatch. They yell, throw objects, and wave their arms to keep the crows away – recently, they started luring them away with Cheetos. Once the chicks have safely hatched, they can use their camouflage and the volunteers go back home. They return to the natural order of things.

Two years after losing Tufters, Jim saw Tacey again. She had two new babies and a new mate who bravely puffed his feathers out, trying to keep Jim away. Tacey herself was flying over a wildlife preserve, across from a nude beach in which Jim had no interest.

A STORM
GATHERS ON THE
COLONY

Paige Bruton

The first fire had been lit two nights before when rioters attacked the pink Goliath that was the Southampton Princess golf club and resort. Two tourists and a hotel engineer had been killed and now, two days of violence later on the Saturday afternoon, the air was thick with the smoke of fires burning across Bermuda.

The young local journalist, Rick Richardson, had arrived on Court Street just as the protestors were firing BB guns and throwing Molotov cocktails at police officers, who responded with teargas. Tethered to his cameraman "like an umbilical cord," he began to film.

Regiment Officer Wendall Hollis stood behind the police line,

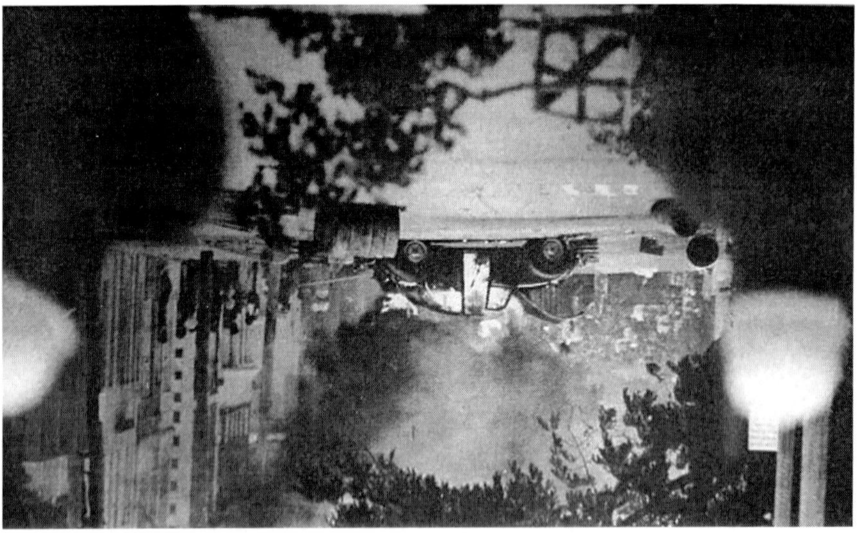

with 24 regiment soldiers at the ready and briefed on the risk they faced to their lives. Arranged as a blockade, rifles heavy in their hands, the soldiers were primed for the possibility of an order to open fire.

Eliyahtsoor Ben Aaharon, who previously went by Melville Saltus, was among the men gathered on Court Street. Leaving his reluctant fiancee in the safety of their home, he was one of the few rioters who was prepared to die for black emancipation on the white-ruled colony.

It was December 3, 1977. Bermuda had never seen a day like this before and never would again.

Rick Richardson, like all local black Bermudians, knew the stakes. He'd been covering violence on the island for the three days since two black men, Erskine "Buck" Burrows and Larry Tacklyn, had been hanged in the island's only male prison early Friday morning. It was the final erection of gallows in the United Kingdom or an overseas territory, and – on the back of the Civil Rights Movement and British abolition of capital punishment – most Bermudians considered the hangings a lynching.

It was particularly warm that afternoon, a clammy heat that makes fruit ripen faster, and the skin sticky with sweat. Rick was relatively green at the local broadcast news station, TV10 News. Even his superiors had shied away from the scene. TV10 was then and until recently a small local station of mostly white foreigners who focused on covering international "rip and read" news – journalist lingo for pre-written stories. He had already heard that a veteran local reporter had had his car torched by activists in similar protests earlier that year, and knew that following the fires was risky.

It was obvious to everyone that Court Street would be the flashpoint of the riots. Everyone, that is, that was in-the-know. Rick's own brother had been on the streets protesting since Thursday night, and kept him up-to-date on any news he had heard. So, he was the only journalist that knew to or was willing to drive up along Court Street that day. CBS and ABC, which had been covering the riots for the last two days, were nowhere to be seen. Rick began to glimpse the backs of the police officers over the crest of the hill. He parked his car, and walked towards the action, telling his cameraman to begin

A STORM GATHERS ON THE COLONY 85

rolling.

"Earlier on we stated that Hamilton had taken on the appearance of a warzone…" he began his report, as screams and BB guns could be heard firing in the background. "Certainly the violence has taken on a new dimension here."

He described the police officers standing in front of him, in white bucket-hats and blue overalls, as well as the sounds of activists shouting "Babylon!" – a biblical city of corruption and immorality – on the other side. The camera zoomed in through the officers' shoulders, focusing on smoke billowing from the metal shell of a Volkswagen Beetle. Hundreds of men lined the street on one side with their backs against the shop fronts and with metal drums strewn across the road. It was to become one of the most iconic images of the riots.

"We have been here on Court Street and witnessed the direct conflict," Rick said as the cameraman moved forward, only steps away from the officers, filming as they loaded their guns with tear gas cartridges, and bursts of red could be seen as they pulled the triggers.

Eliyahtsoor Ben Aaharon had already been on Court Street that day as the number of Black protesters began to swell. Considered the heart of the poorer "Back-A-Town" neighborhood of Hamilton, the road was named for the Supreme Court building, whose imposing clocktower commemorating a birthday of Queen Victoria cast a shadow over the neighborhood. Even now white parents like mine warn their children that this is one of Hamilton's dangerous areas. The road is still gated by a square where disenfranchised men often loiter, where cheap boutique clothing stores and hair salons line the road, and where the headquarters of the historically black-supported Progressive Labour Party resides.

The Youth Wing of the Progressive Labor Party was an important recruitment funnel for the Black Power group Eliyahtsoor had formed eight years earlier: The Black Beret Cadre. In 1969, along with three of his friends: Ewart Brown, Philip Perinchief and John "Dionne" Bassett, Eliyahtsoor gathered to read and discuss the teachings of Malcolm X, Fidel Castro and Eldridge Cleaver of the Black Panthers, whom they had been introduced to at universities in both the United Kingdom and the United States. Mirrored in the texts, Eliyahtsoor recognized his own mistreatment that he had suffered as a black man in one of the richest countries of the world but whose fortune was and is controlled by a white minority.

Eliyahtsoor was therefore unsurprised by the violent actions of hundreds of black men since the final appeal to save Buck Burrows and Larry Tacklyn failed. They were his friends, and were often present at the meetings of the Black Berets, well known on a small, but still racially segregated, island.

That afternoon the street was becoming crowded, and men started breaking into the local black-owned businesses and looting around him. Eliyahtsoor spotted the burning VW through the crowd and knew it was likely that the driver had been beaten and then fled – he had helped a couple the day before escape their vehicle unscathed, after which he and a group of men set it on fire. It was only a matter of time before the police arrived.

"I was tired of the dispossessed destroying their own neighborhoods," he later said. Men had entered the Progressive Labour Party headquarters, and Eliyahtsoor closed the doors encouraging the men to go home. He knew that the rioting had become out of control, and that there was the possibility that the entirety of Hamilton would be lit on fire.

Officer Wendell Hollis had just come back to the Regiment's Warwick Camp in the early hours of Saturday morning, having spent the night guarding firemen who were extinguishing a fire at a nearby hair salon. Wendell was exhausted; he had just flown in from the US after being called to duty due to the widespread civil unrest.

His cousin, Colonel Brendan Hollis, briefed him on the dire situation on Court Street. It seemed that police officers would unlikely hold back the crowds for long, and Wendell had been selected to command a riot squad who would offer police support on the front line.

The Royal Bermuda Regiment is the island's home army, and until 2018 it conscripted every Bermudian man for three years of training every second week. This was abolished and recruitment was made voluntary after criticism likened the forced service of black men under often white leaders to slavery, particularly when the Regiment is considered by many to be a representation of the British Crown in Bermuda.

A colony since its discovery in 1609, Bermuda had no native inhabitants, and British sailors on their way to the New World established a settlement based on African slave labor. Wendell, a newly-promoted white lieutenant and lawyer, could trace his family history in Bermuda back to 1619. He joined the Regiment after his university studies in 1976, one year before the riots, and he had been promoted to officer five months earlier.

By the time Wendell joined the Regiment, the climate in Bermuda was already tense. Buck Burrows and Larry Tacklyn had already been arrested for the assassination of the Governor Richard Sharples, the British representative on the island and head of the Regiment, his aide-de-camp Hugh Sayers, the British Police Commissioner George Duckett, as well as Victor Rego and Mark Doe in the so-called "Supermarket Murders". Burrows took a vow of silence after the arrest, writing that his motive was "to show that these colonists were just ordinary people like ourselves, who eat, sleep and die just like anybody else and that we need not stand in fear and awe of them."

Wendell himself was against capital punishment but followed the orders of his superiors to try and restore order. Under his command 24 men arrived at Court Street from Warwick Camp. Though unrest had been growing since the murders, the Regiment was not well-equipped – symbolic of a sleepy white establishment who could not see that there was anything in rich and beautiful Bermuda to be angry about. Their self-loading rifles were dated and not meant for riots but for a warzone. Wendell was terrified that if something went wrong, rioters would be the ones to pick up the weapons.

When he and his platoon arrived on Court Street, Wendell was nervous but determined – everyone except two of his men agreed to risk their lives and stand behind the police, and he had complete trust in them. The platoon began beating their riot shields as they approached the back of the officers. Once in formation, Wendell was astounded at the scene in front of him: around 500 protestors armed with sticks, machetes and throwing Molotov cocktails were beginning to advance around the burning car that separated the ten police officers from the crowds. The officers fired rubber bullets, which from such a short range were "enough to break someone's shoulder" recalled Eliyahtsoor, who heard the bullets ricocheting off the roofs around him.

A dark and heavy storm cloud was gathering overhead, making the action feel more claustrophobic than ever. Eliyahtsoor decided that the protesting was no longer safe, his friends and brothers were angry, but that in the chaos no real change would be achieved. He left the riots to return to his fiancee and young son, his back against the rioters who were now throwing Molotov cocktails by the dozen.

Rick was unaware of exactly how violent the confrontation had become. He moved up alongside the officers, filming down the line as they fired rubber bullets. He'd been concentrating on covering as much of the scene as possible in his broadcast, telling his cameraman what shots he was missing in his colleague's nervousness.

"Rick Richardson for TV10 News on the corner of Court and Victoria –" at that moment Rick had been hit by a Molotov cocktail to the leg, which miraculously did not explode, but Rick knew he had pushed his luck. "Let's get out of here, let's get out of here!" he shouted, as he could be heard running in the broadcast. Suddenly, another searing pain against his leg, and Rick was hit by a ball bearing. Fifty years later Rick is still coy: "If I'm truthful … there was a bit of fear," he said with a smile, and then described how he immediately left for his TV station to have the film processed.

As Rick ran past Wendell, the officer became increasingly worried. The protestors were becoming more violent and he didn't believe that they could be held back much longer. Just then, another police officer drove up on a moped and asked Wendell whether or not he had noticed the sky.

Wendell looked above him. What he thought had been the sun setting was in fact the enclosing darkness of a storm cloud hovering. Suddenly, shots were fired from a house near the officers, and the rioters were close enough to the police and the Regiment that both sides were able to recognize one another. On a small island the violence was between the two groups was a violence between neighbors, between friends. The local supermarket cashier, the gas station attendant, the officer he serves weekly at the local bar – they locked eyes, knowing that it was the symbols they embodied rather than the bodies of individuals that had led to such a feeling of betrayal.

Wendell and his men knew that they had now become targets. Then the rains broke.

In Bermuda the rainstorm that ended the riots is now more legend than historical fact. Wendell said it was "Biblical," and saw the large, heavy droplets as a divine intervention to protect the safety of Bermudians. He describes how the street was turned into a river and his boots filled with water. My great aunt and uncle would later shrug saying "you know that Bermudians just hate rain." Regardless, the rioters dissipated. The British had been called for backup and the following day hundreds of soldiers arrived by plane from fighting in the Troubles in Northern Ireland. People were afraid. The Crown had played its hand.

For my aunt and uncle, as well as many other white Bermudians, they thought that the rioting in December 1977 was a waste of life. It's true that there has never been such violence again. In 1995, there was a nationwide referendum on independence from the United Kingdom. People voted to remain a colony. The following year Eliyahtsoor left the island, believing that there was no hope for change. He moved to Ghana, hoping to build a nation state for black men and women who had been kidnaped as part of the slave trade. He is still hoping for a new Israel. Meanwhile, Philip Perinchief, his friend and another founding member of the Black Beret Cadre served as the island's Attorney General from 2006-2007, Ewart Brown of the Black Berets became the island's Premier in 2006. He was later charged with 13 counts of corruption in 2021, his reputation in Bermuda tarnished.

Wendell Hollis was promoted to Second Lieutenant of the Regiment and now serves on their Board of Directors as well as being a practicing lawyer at one of the island's top law firms. He hopes to retire to one of his properties, and write a book about his experiences.

Rick Richardson became one of the most successful and recognizable faces in Bermuda for his journalism. He later worked in New York, but returned to Bermuda, which he could never be too far from. "I was just doing my job," he said. "But people still come up to me and jokingly mimic my running from the scene. I'm famous here."

Though he may be a hero now to some, for white Bermudians like my great aunt and uncle, they dismissed this, saying "everyone had forgotten about the riots by Christmas."

THE PALACE OF MADNESS

Luwa (Elena) Yin

It was Halloween and I was looking for ghost stories when I stumbled upon a photograph that would tell a story more frightening than any I could have imagined.

The photo was of a postcard. It showed a big, three-story building, topped with an American flag. It was surrounded by manicured grounds and along a footpath where people walked. The women held parasols. At the bottom were the words: Bloomingdale Asylum for the Insane. The postcard seemed to be sending a message. Just as the parasols were protecting the women from the sun, so too was the asylum protecting the people strolling outside from those who lived within.

BLOOMINGDALE ASYLUM.

BLOOMINGDALE ASYLUM FOR THE INSANE.

But life inside the Bloomingdale Asylum largely remained a mystery until the late 19th century – until a young journalist decided to see for himself what it felt like to be a patient.

He emerged with a ghost story to tell.

The Bloomingdale Asylum was chartered in 1771, and the main building was completed in 1821. It was massive – 210 feet long and 60 feet wide. It was built from brownstone. Thomas Taylor, who oversaw the construction, said that the building should have the appearance of a palace rather than a jail. It was located in northern Manhattan, between Broadway and Amsterdam Ave., close enough to the Hudson to allow residents a view of the river. Landscape architects designed the grounds, covering them with trees. On one side was a vegetable garden so that patients might have nutritious food as well as an outdoor activity.

The plan was to provide more humane treatment for the insane who, for centuries, had been confined to unspeakably cruel and awful institutions.

The most complete and chilling account of life inside the Bloomingdale Asylum came from a young journalist named Julius Chambers, a correspondent for the *New York Tribune*.

He had just turned 21 when in an act of journalistic bravery – some might say bravado – he got himself admitted to the asylum by pretending to be mentally ill.

There were two major buildings for patients. One, called "the Lodge," housed patients judged to be more violent and dangerous. This was where Chambers ended up.

At his admission, he went through a cursory medical examination. His money and some of his jewelry were taken, and after that, he was led down a dimly lit hallway illuminated by a single gas jet.

He passed through an iron door and saw his room. He would later write that it was more like a cell, not more than eight feet wide and 10 feet long. The only piece of furniture was a straw cot, and the only light came from the gas jet in the hallway. The window was directly above his straw cot, and warm air blew in during the summer.

THE PALACE OF MADNESS 95

The door of the room did not have a knob, and the wall was unbreakable. His room was the "most uninviting" place.

He was told to remove his shoes and clothes before going to sleep. He could smell the chlorine of lime mixed with water. It was so strong that it gave him a headache. He had trouble sleeping for days.

Every morning, the door of his room was thrown open, and he was woken for breakfast. He and the other patients would eat on a rough wooden table. On his first day in the asylum, he had only a cup of tea and a small roll. The sugar bowl had ants in it. He still felt hungry after swallowing everything in.

The nights at the asylum were not restful. His sleep was interrupted by the sound of slamming.

One night he heard a piercing yell coming from the basement. That was where the more violent patients were housed. Someone was screaming in agony. It would stop and then start again. As darkness descended, the screaming died down. In its place was a constant hissing and groaning.

This was one of many nights Chambers spent trembling and hoping for dawn to come.

The patients ranged in age from 19 to 79. Only one or two were not considered dangerous. One was said to have bitten another patient because he didn't like him. Another had gained a reputation for kicking "the head off" another person in the same building. The medical examinations were cursory. Patients had their pulse taken and asked one question: "How do you feel this morning?"

In 1876, Julius Chambers published *A Mad World and Its People*.

A haunting tale, and hardly a ghost story.

UNDROWNING

Isabella Anahí García-Méndez

Crazy Rich Asians changed my life.

On a Saturday afternoon in August 2019, my mom and I went to see *Crazy Rich Asians*. I thought I was just seeing a movie about a wealthy family. I was about to learn something unsettling about my own.

The next morning, we went to Mass with my brother. My dad was out of town. The homily focused on living in one's truth – an eerie echo of the movie we had seen the day before. Maybe it was the movie, maybe it was the homily, or maybe it was the combination of the two, but when we got home my mother hesitated before getting out of the car.

"I have to tell you something," she said. It had something to do with the movie.

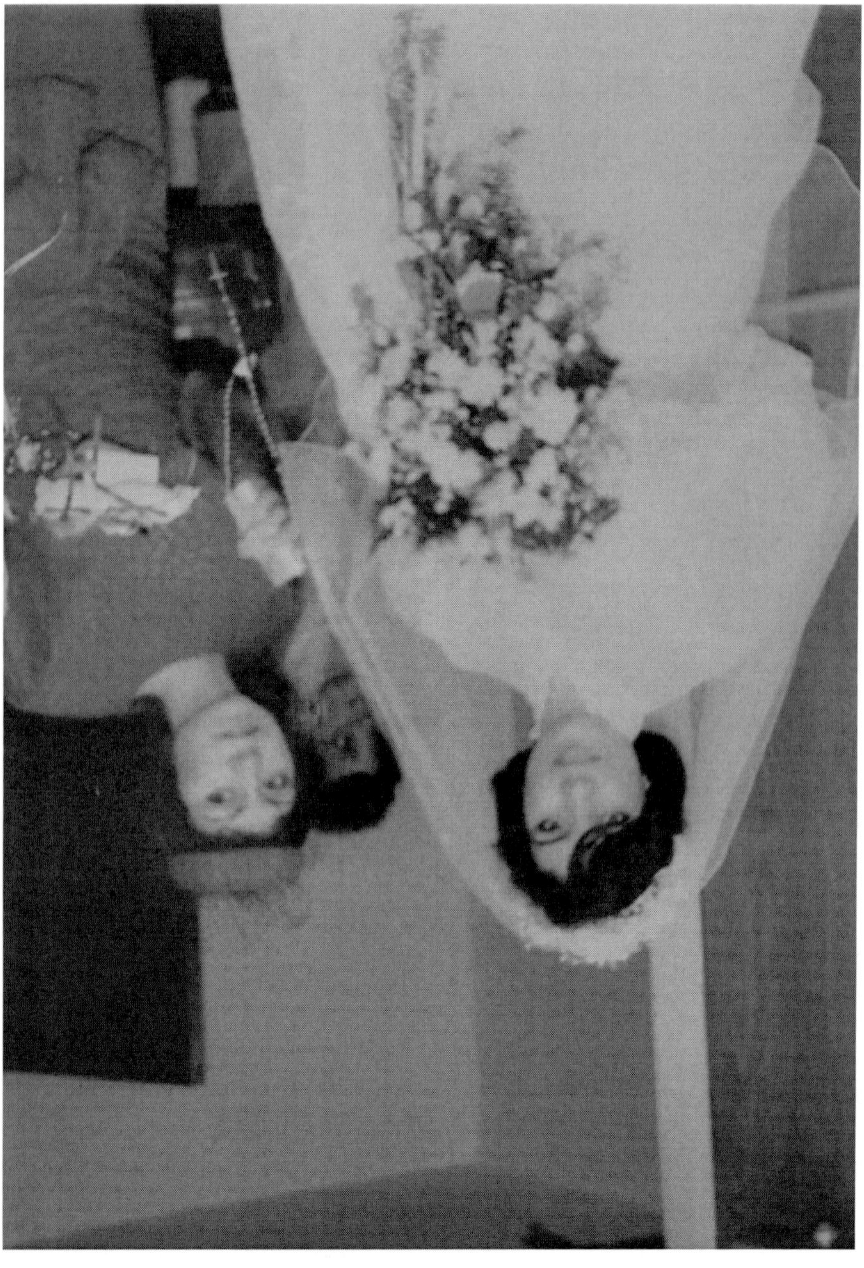

"Do you have another child?" I asked.

She shook her head no. She was making me guess.

"Were you married before?"

I come from a very large family. I have over 100 first and second cousins. My mom is the youngest of 14 siblings. She and her family came to the Central Valley of California from Mexico when she was about to enter high school. My dad is the youngest of 11 siblings, all of whom live in or near Mexico City. My dad was the only one to move to the United States when he was 23 years old. They met each other on a dance floor in Stockton, California.

My parents' marriage is so perfect, it makes every relationship I've had so far seem lesser. They never fight. They are wonderfully supportive parents. They are terrific to watch on a dance floor. They do all the housework together, even the laundry and cooking. They like to sit outside in the backyard they designed based on all their favorite resorts and gardens from around the world. They built it together.

We are devout Catholics and attend Mass every Sunday morning. When my brother and I weren't singing in the choir, playing handbells for special Masses, or helping as altar servers, the four of us would sit together, holding hands as we prayed the "Our Father".

My mom was a catechism teacher and after our First Communions, my brother and I would line up for the consecrated bread and wine each week. My dad never went up with us, but my mom did occasionally, crossing her arms across her chest to signify that, while she wanted the priest's blessing, she couldn't take the Eucharist. My parents weren't married through the church. I never questioned why.

We woke on Saturday mornings to music blasting through the house. But unlike most Mexican families, the soundtrack was not strictly Mexican. My dad played Brazilian bossa nova, Edith Piaf, and Mexican rock.

My mom opted for Latino dance hits. She also liked Arabic music.

My mom nodded yes. My brother and I gasped softly.

She began to tell us her story. She insisted that she had not wanted her first marriage to be a secret. In fact, she had left little clues for us everywhere. We just had to see them.

The secret, she told us, began with my dad's mother, my *abuelita*. She had asked my parents not to tell anyone about the marriage. My mom honored her wishes even after she died in 2018. We don't know why my *abuelita* asked my parents to keep the secret. My dad thinks it was to protect them. My mom thinks it was out of shame. Now, sitting in the car, she told us that she had been true to her promise. But my *abuelita* was gone and now my mom was no longer bound by secrecy.

She told us she was not ashamed of her first marriage and never asked anyone on her side of the family to keep it secret. So all my aunts, uncles, cousins, and their spouses not only knew about my mom's first marriage, they were at her wedding. They knew the first husband. They knew about the divorce.

And for 21 years, nobody let it slip. Not once.

I am a curious person, nosy even. Over the years I would hear whispers and snippets of family secrets, though I never knew the full stories. And I never heard so much as a murmur about a marriage before my parents'.

So I needed to know why all these people kept the story of the marriage a secret from my brother and me. And there was something else: how did they manage to do it?

My mom met a man in her early 20s. She was studying to become a teacher. He was a young Pakistani man studying to become a doctor. She found him fascinating. He was handsome, ambitious, and so different from anybody else she knew.

They began dating, and three years later he wanted to get married. She did not. She did, however, want to do things the right way and honor her Catholic parents, so she agreed to marry him.

The first husband did not speak Spanish. My *Tio* Pedro, who spoke English, translated when the first husband and his mother came to my grandparents' home to ask for permission to marry my mom. My grandparents had their reservations but they consented. She had to convince the priest to marry them because the first husband was Muslim.

My mom believed she had the support of her family. What she didn't know is that my aunts and uncles felt they had no choice but to accept my grandparents' decision to approve of the marriage. My *Tio* Cruz, one of my mom's older brothers, never liked the man. He thought he was too serious for my mom because my family was fun and lively. My *tio* was also suspicious of his intentions with my mom. He never said this to my mom or my grandparents, but he and my other uncles would talk about their concerns privately.

My aunts worried about what the marriage would look like. They were concerned that the cultural, religious, and language differences could make things difficult for them as a couple.

Everyone kept their thoughts to themselves. My mom did not learn until much later that her parents wept the morning of the wedding.

My mom was a legal resident and the first husband insisted she apply for citizenship so she could sponsor him. Eventually, they sponsored his mother, his brother, and his sister as well. They all lived together in Merced. The marriage would last seven years.

My aunts and uncles who didn't speak English remember the first husband sitting on the couch reading books during the weekly family gatherings at my grandparents' home. They felt that he was just playing the role of a good husband. He would occasionally talk with my uncles and my young cousins who spoke English. One of my aunts believed he was putting on a show, knowing the marriage would not last, and never truly trying to become part of the family.

My mom told us how the first husband's younger siblings were in high school and were struggling to fit in after arriving from Pakistan. His younger sister was getting bullied at school for having hairy legs. The younger brother was very religious, and when he found out his sister shaved her legs, he blamed my mom and he held a knife to her throat.

My mom's closest sisters knew her life at home was less than perfect, but they didn't know how bad it was. At one point, my mom thought she was pregnant. Overwhelmed with excitement, she shared the news with the first husband. He immediately took her to the lab where he was working to get a pregnancy test. She recalled that he seemed relieved when the test came back negative. She didn't understand why her husband wouldn't be excited at the thought of them having a baby together.

One day, my mom got a call from her principal. He was calling to let her know that the staff meeting the following day had been moved to another time. After giving her the update, he asked "By the way, did you change your number?"

Confused, my mom said no and asked why. He explained that he had called the number he had on file for her and that the first husband answered. He told my mom's principal to call a different number in order to reach my mom.

As soon as they hung up, my mom dialed what she thought was her own number. The first husband answered. He hung up and came home and that was when she discovered that he had transferred their number to an apartment he was secretly renting on the other side of town. He told her he had gotten it for his mother.

She threw him out, believing the apartment was for another woman. She called my *abuelita* and my godmother, my *nina*. They immediately went to her house and comforted her. She felt betrayed and heartbroken. But more than anything, she was embarrassed to have company when her house wasn't immaculately clean. My *nina* remembers my *abuelita* insisting that my mom come home with her. She refused, so the three women spent the night sleeping in the same bed.

My mother filed for divorce. Many in her family were unaware. They did notice, however, that they no longer saw the first husband around.

A few months after her divorce, my mom's gynecologist mentioned she had another patient with the same last name as my mom. That's how my mom found out the first husband had remarried. To this day she doesn't know for sure if his second wife was in the picture during their marriage.

Ask any of my relatives why my mom got a divorce and you will hear different answers: He only used her for her citizenship. He took advantage of her. He was engaged to a woman back in Pakistan the whole time.

Though devout Catholics, they all supported her divorce and felt relieved when it happened. It turned out they were familiar with failed marriages, and would become even more so in the next generation. Not that anyone talked about it. Ever.

My mom, I learned, was not the first. Two of her brothers were also divorced. Back when they still lived in Mexico, one of her brothers had moved in with his partner without getting married. The local priest found this unacceptable and blamed my *abuelita*, prohibiting her from taking Communion. She was humiliated and made it clear to her other children that marriage through the church was a family requirement. That's why it was so important that my mom did things the "right way". Her other brother had a daughter from his first marriage, though he never kept this hidden from the children of his second marriage.

It was not as if we were all strangers to one another. When my maternal grandparents were alive, dozens of us gathered every week at their home. *Carne asada* and conversation glued us together. The men mostly stayed outside, grilling, drinking beers, and listening to music. Inside, the women prepared the side dishes and chatted.

I liked rotating from room to room, picking up on the bits and pieces of personal tragedies, triumphs, infidelity, betrayal, disrespect, loss, and scandal. Yet I never knew the full stories. I would gather clues, often in the form of advice. I remember my late aunt once telling me, "Never let a man disrespect you like this, *mija*". I didn't know what *this* meant. After my grandparents died, the weekly family get-togethers died with them.

But as I grew older, I heard and understood more. Several of my cousins were unhappy in their love lives. I was too young to share their confidence. I assumed they had other people to talk to. Who was I to ask?

It turns out, we all thought that way. Fearful of intruding upon each other's lives and privacy, we never asked questions. Sometimes not even to ask if someone was okay.

After my mom told her secret, I began to ask my relatives about their versions of the story. What I also began to hear were stories of secrets of their own. I heard stories about betrayal and abuse and what lays behind "they're not together anymore."

Desahogar, a verb in Spanish, translates to venting, freeing, or unburdening oneself of something. However, its literal translation is "to undrown." The literal translation speaks to what would happen to you if you didn't vent, or *desahogarte*. You would drown, trying to hold it all in.

We left our loved ones to drown in their own truths. Shocking as my mom's story was, it soon got lost in a sea of family secrets.

My mom never wanted to drown in the secret she kept from us. She left us clues.

The photo album from her first wedding was right next to our family photo albums that I would frequently look through. But somehow I never noticed it. There were also children's books from her first years of teaching that bore her name from her first marriage.

One day when I was young, my parents took us to a house where I'd never been before. The house was empty and all I would remember was that it was there that my cousins, who had come along, taught me to blow bubble gum bubbles. I saw no reason to ask why there was nothing in the house, not in the rooms or the closets. I was focused on blowing bubbles.

Somehow it was made clear that my mother owned this house and that she was preparing to sell it. In the nature of my family–my parents, my brother, my godparents, and my cousins–had all come along to help. Perhaps I was too young, but I did not ask why she owned a house if we already had one.

The house, I now see, held great symbolic importance for her. She had had the money to buy the first husband out when their marriage ended. The house represented independence for my mother, freedom from an unhappy marriage, and freedom to meet someone new.

LETTING KISHAN GO

Mansi Vithlani

On the last day of my brother's life all I could think about were the six months I had missed with him. How I missed the first time he walked up the stairs after eight months of being unable to. How I missed the countless hospitalizations leading up to his death. How I missed being able to massage his arms and legs when they were hurting more than normal. How I missed the day he found out he was not strong enough for a heart transplant. How I missed the shift in his personality from bubbly to heartbreakingly quiet.

But he waited. He waited until I returned home from New York. He gifted me 27 days. That was all I had before saying goodbye. There were many things I wanted to tell him. Goodbye was not one of them.

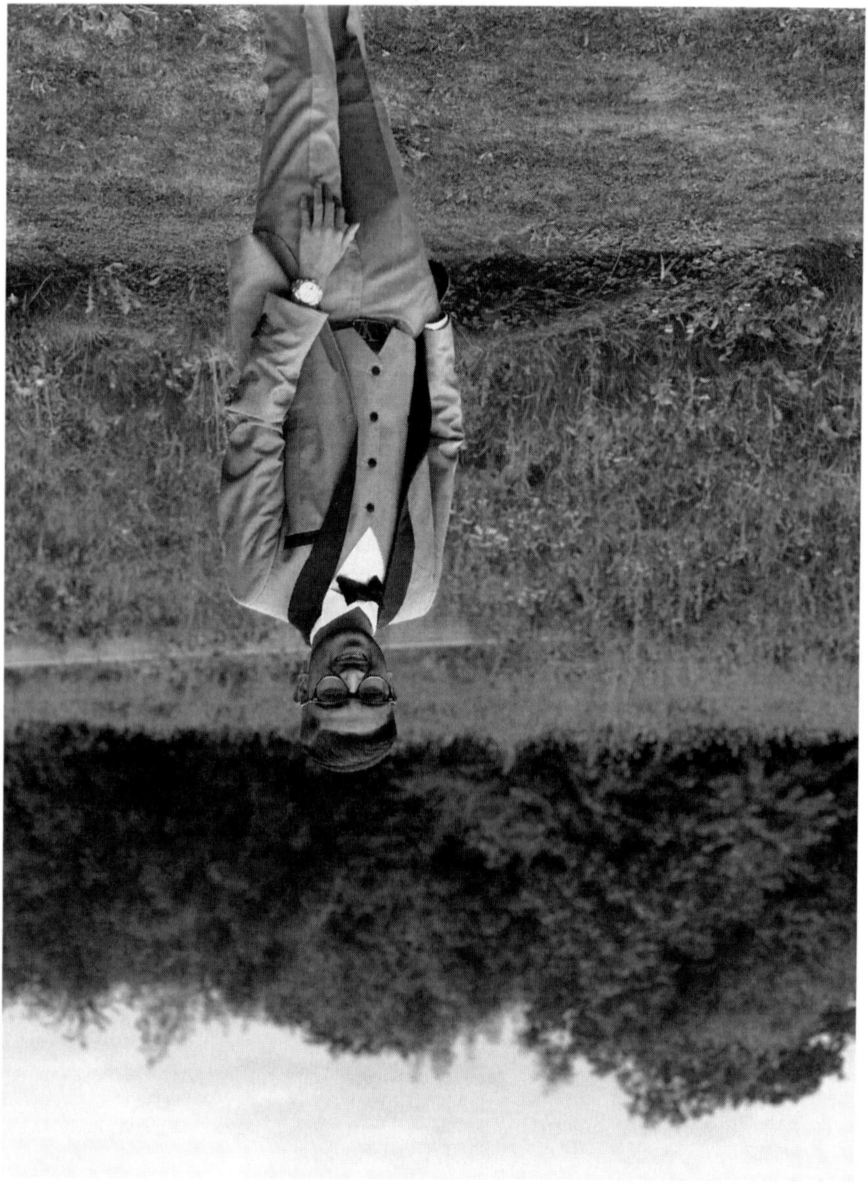

Perhaps he anticipated his end. He did not prepare me. But he did accept it.

My brother's name is Kishan Shayam Vithlani. He was 26 years old. Arsenal fanatic. A computer genius. My eldest brother.

He was or he is. I interchange between the two. I am aware that he *is* still present with me. But it seems preferable to state "he was" to strangers.

He was born on January 23, 1996. Four months later he was diagnosed with a congenital heart condition. Simply put, he was born with half a heart. The medical jargon is exceedingly overwhelming to explain.

Brace yourself.

He had a right isomerism. A common atrium. A double outlet right ventricle. A complete atrio ventricular septal defect. A univentricular connection to morphological right ventricle and rudimentary left ventricle. A double outlet right ventricle pulmonary stenosis, valvar and subvalvar. An anomalous pulmonary drainage to right SVC right atrial junction. An asplenia.

Hard to explain and too much to understand. But none of this defined him. Kishan did not live his illness.

It was not until March 1996 that my parents received his primary cardiac diagnosis. Kishan went into hospital at three months to receive his immunizations. A routine appointment that most babies have at that age. "We thought he was normal," my mum says.

But then my mum and dad's whole world changed. Their first-born child was uncommonly sick. The general practitioners informed my parents that Kishan had to be admitted immediately at the Leicester Royal Infirmary.

"His heart," the doctor said. "It's not right."

Kishan was one of a million children with this diagnosis at the time. It was the start of a never-ending series of scans and procedures. When first diagnosed, his life expectancy was estimated to be around 30 years. My parents were informed that he could live longer or shorter.

Kishan was three months old when he was admitted to the Glenfield Hospital, the leading cardiology hospital in the UK at the time.

It was also where Kishan would spend his last few days.

I frequently wonder when Kishan realized he was born unwell. Perhaps not at the time of his initial big surgery when he was five months old? But maybe after the second part of that operation a few years later? Or maybe as a teenager when he was taking more than 20 medical tablets each day.

The first operation, the Fontan procedure, is a type of open-heart surgery – *a bilateral bidirectional Glenn Shunts and reimplantation of pulmonary veins into the right atrium.*

"He was a normal happy baby," my mum says. "It was a hidden sickness." Her name is Priti and, yes she is very pretty. She remembers feeling frightened and unsure of what would happen when they brought him into the operating room.

The second part came when Kishan was five years old: *Completion of Total Cavo Pulmonary Connection using extra cardiac conduit. This operation is done by attaching a tube of a special plastic (a conduit of Gore-Tex) from the lower body vein (Inferior Vena Cava) to the base of the lung artery (Pulmonary Artery) diverting blue (deoxygenated) blood away from the heart straight to the lungs.*

A hole (fenestration) may be created between the tube and the right collecting chamber (Right Atrium). As with the Internal Fontan there can be a rise in pressure in the lung arteries after surgery and the hole acts as a pressure valve.

But in between the first and the second procedures, my parents did the expected baby things with him.

They went to softplay. He began kindergarten. He started going to primary school. During this five year period, my other brother Dilan was born.

"His milestones were slower than a normal baby," my mum says. "He never met his milestones and didn't start walking until he was two."

Kishan's life became more complicated after the second surgery. His heart operation was successful. But the fluid was not draining properly. Additional drains were installed. His lungs collapsed. He was hospitalized for seven weeks.

But afterwards he led a normal life with a few restrictions. No riding fast roller coasters. Or participating in contact sports. Or traveling anywhere where there are mosquitos or high infection rates. Or eating spinach. That was something to do with his Vitamin K.

Kishan, however, was a rule breaker. He did take part in sports. He was a tennis player. He was an ambitious cricketer. He would play soccer in the living room. That would irritate our dad. And the neighbors too if the ball was kicked or batted into their garden.

I don't recall him being this active in a long time. Particularly throughout his early twenties.

I have trouble recalling what I was doing the day before Kishan passed. It was Thursday January 12, 2023. And then we lost him on Friday the 13th. That could mean something to the superstitious. But for me it made me think of his birthday. January 23, ten days away.

Thirteen and 23 also reminded me of the three of us. Kishan, Dilan and Mansi. Eldest to youngest. Three threes. It flowed so well.

Kishan the leader.

Dilan the level-headed one.

And me, the baby.

Growing up, I watched them play on their PlayStation, affixed to the screen and glued together at the waist. They liked to play FIFA, the soccer game. They would start to play as soon as they got home from school, still wearing their uniforms – a black pullover with a white a polo. Twins. Our mum would call them for dinner and they would not hear her. They would purposely ignore her. She would spoon the food into their mouths as they played. It was usually dhal and rice. I cannot remember the last time we three ate dinner together. They played FIFA into adulthood. Soccer was Kishan's world. Dilan's too. But they did not support the same teams. Arsenal was everything to Kishan and Manchester United to Dilan. One of the biggest rivalries of the British Premier League. One of Dilan's first games with Kish was a match between the two.

One of our last outings as a trio was two weeks before Kishan passed away. To a soccer game on Boxing Day, December 26th. Of course we went to see Arsenal. Not Manchester United. Kishan and

I never went there. I wasn't even supposed to go on this occasion. My cousin had pulled out. So I went. Maybe it was fate that I went. Arsenal won.

Later that week Dilan took Kish to an evening game. Now he is filled with regret because Kishan had a nasty cough that night. It was only later that we discovered it was a severe chest infection. Dilan encouraged Kishan to go to the hospital and miss the game.

Kishan would not have it. Dilan recalls Kish saying, "no, no, let's go on Friday, because I want to go to the Arsenal game". But maybe, he thinks, had Kish spent an additional day or two in the hospital, the antibiotics would have kicked in sooner.

"But I think he also knew at that point that things were going to get hard," Dilan says.

"And that's why he wanted to go to this Arsenal game."

The game ended in a scoreless tie. Dilan returned to Manchester for university. I was in Leicester preparing for my return to New York to complete my master's, the degree that Kish pushed me to apply for. I was scheduled to depart on Friday the 13th.

The Friday before, Kishan went to Glenfield Hospital for a scan. The hospital wanted to admit him for his chest infection but there were no open beds. He waited until after the weekend. On Monday he was admitted.

That week I went to the hospital everyday to see him. He still had the nasty cough that was not improving. I could hear his cough down the hall.

Kishan was not talking much. This was out of character. Kishan was the sort of talker who started conversations and kept them going. But now he would sleep, a lot. I would nap in the chair beside him. He spoke little in the last weeks of his life. Company was enough. I regret not recognizing it as a sign at the time.

We didn't have many long talks before his final days. Kishan lacked the strength. We did, briefly, discuss this story. It was Wednesday January 11. I summoned the courage to ask him if I could tell his story. He agreed without hesitation or questions. We had no idea it would become a story he'd never read.

That Wednesday was also the day I noticed how different his eyes looked. He was of course unwell. But his eyes looked different – wider and glassy. His pupils would fixate and he would stare blankly. I told my mum. She thought his eyes looked normal. I recall telling one of Kishan's doctors about the change. He didn't seem to notice a change, either.

My mum and dad never told us Kishan was so sick when he was born. Dilan can't recall the moment that our parents told us. It was not a family meeting type of thing. I am certain there was not an occasion to mark it. We both figured it out as we grew up.

Kishan had requested soup the day before he passed. It was vegetable soup. Soup was one of the meals he frequently craved and that he was able to keep down in his final months. Even so, I would not have given it much thought at the time. He liked the way my grandma or my mum made it. Not too much pepper. None at all most of the time. He couldn't take the spice anymore.

So I brought the soup to the hospital. I parked in the South Entrance. I forgot to place a ticket on the windshield. No one was going to check anyway. They never did.

Kish. I prefer to refer to him as such. Kishy as well. He had shifted wards. But this time it was closer to the South Entrance. The CCU, the Critical Care Unit. I was holding his soup in a flask and stir-fried noodles for my parents. I tried not to worry about the ward's ominous sounding name. Kishan passing did not cross my mind at this point.

We were upstairs the day before. Kishan was in a side room on Ward 32 – the cardiac investigations day case ward. I was always getting lost on my route to that ward. Now I ask myself, what had happened over 24 hours to remand him to the critical care unit?

I remember stepping in and seeing Chris, his primary nurse. Kishan had been moved from the pediatric facility to the adult clinic when he turned 16. That is where we met Chris. Kishan's favorite nurse. Mum's too.

"I think it was just his personality that captured his heart," she says. Kishan, of course, was an easy patient. He was charming, hardly overwhelmed by his never-ending appointments. He was content to let the nurses get on with their job. Often he would outsmart them.

Kish was well-versed in his illness.

Chris was very patient, but could also be direct. He would always make himself available when Kishan needed him, as well as for my mum when she would bombard him with questions and worries.

At around 19, Kish was admitted to the intensive care unit with life-threatening sepsis. His mobility deteriorated. He also became exceedingly thin and frail. This happened twice.

"They told us that we may have to put him on dialysis. That he may not make it. His kidneys were failing at that point," my mum says. But within 24 hours things improved. A "miracle" she called it.

This was the moment at which Kishan recognized he needed to be more cautious about his health. He understood that his body was more susceptible to infection. It was a revelation that he needed to make the most of his time.

So Kishan started a bucket list. We began crossing things off: driving down Highway 1 in California. We visited Vancouver and Niagara Falls. He bought last minute tickets to see Kendrick Lamar perform live in Toronto. He would meticulously arrange these trips so that Dilan and I could go with him.

My parents did everything to make his bucket list happen. It was endless. "He didn't want people to brand him as poorly," says my mum. "And to be fair, a lot of people didn't know he had a heart condition, only the people that were close to him."

My mum frequently slept in Kishan's hospital rooms, sometimes winding up in a plastic chair next to Kish's bed if there was no recliner. Sometimes she would sleep only for an hour. Then she would return home to prepare meals for him and the rest of the family.

"I've always been lucky I was allowed to stay with him," she says. "Wherever he was, especially when he became an adult. It was very difficult for them to say yes, but they did."

But when Kishan had sepsis the hospital would not let her stay in the ICU. But one night Kishan was so unsettled that they phoned my mum in the early hours of the morning, urging her to return. She was permitted to remain in the intensive care section.

I recall going to see him once while he was in the hospital with sepsis. He questioned why I wasn't at school. It was 8:30 at night. He believed it to be dawn. He did not want me skipping class to see him.

We spent one of Dilan's birthdays in the ICU. We were all there, mum, dad, grandma, Dilan and I. We bought a birthday cake and lit the candles. Dilan discreetly blew them out. But we got caught. We set the fire alarm off. The nurses told us off. But Kishan would have wanted to celebrate Dilan's birthday. Even if he couldn't recall the events.

Kishan went to Leicester University when he was 18. In his second year he once again developed sepsis. He spent five weeks in the hospital after two weeks in the ICU. He then had to relearn how to walk. He was walking close to normal after four months. Still, Kishan graduated with a first class degree and went to work as a software developer.

During the pandemic Kishan was shielded at home for about 18 months. It was also the time where managing his protein was crucial. Kishan's health began to deteriorate again at the start of 2022, especially in light of the effects of the pandemic on his mental health. He grew depressed but would not admit it. But we saw.

Finally, in May of 2022 we took our first family holiday in a long time to Dubai. But by now Kishan's health was not good. His legs were filled with fluid. They resembled balloons. He lacked the stamina to continuously walk, so we pushed him in a wheelchair. Although the doctor said he could travel, looking back maybe we shouldn't have.

Still, the tech whiz that he was, Kishan devised futuristic activities. He purchased admission to the *Museum of the Future.* Kishan decided to go for a quick stroll to stretch his legs. We were leaving the museum at this point. He didn't enjoy being constrained to his wheelchair. My mum was with my grandma, who was likewise confined to a wheelchair. Dilan was hailing a cab. I was dumping trash in the bin. My dad was pushing the empty wheelchair.

We hadn't been paying attention to Kishan. He had no idea that amongst the access ramp there was a step. He fell flat on his front. But there was no sound. When my dad turned around he saw Kish on the ground.

We didn't realize how badly he hurt himself until we picked him up and saw he had cut both of his knees and his elbow. The wounds were severe. There was blood everywhere. His flesh was ripped.

The museum called for an ambulance. We had no clue how the healthcare system functioned. At the hospital Kish was given warfarin to avoid blood clots. He was smiling as they stitched him up, 29 stitches in total, both knees and his elbow.

That fall changed Kishan's life. Afterwards he slept in our living room with my mum and dad. His fluid regulation worsened. He spent the bulk of that summer in the hospital with cellulitis and suspected sepsis.

We removed his bed from his bedroom and reorganized the living room. My parents were the best caregivers. One slept on a pop-up bed, while the other slept on the sofa. They would frequently rotate places. My dad would wake up with Kish in the middle of the night. If Kish's legs hurt, he'd massage them. When Kish couldn't sleep, they'd have late-night talks. They were both never far from his side.

"He was my bestie," my mum says. "He trusted me more than anybody else in the family."

Kishan's demeanor began to shift in September 2022. He started to become quiet. More reserved. Ever less active.

He then received this letter. It read.

I am writing regarding this young gentleman with Fontan's associated liver disease, liver cirrhosis with preserved liver function and evidence of liver lesions suspicious for a hepatocellular cancer on recent MRI scan and TACE protocol CT. Case has been discussed at the HPB MDT. Kishan would not be fit for surgery because of his liver condition and background comorbidities but would be a potential candidate for TACE.

My mum called me in New York two days after my birthday to tell me that Kishan had suspected cancer. I burst into tears.

Yet for weeks I had had a feeling something was wrong. He was going to the hospital more frequently. I was not there. I should have been there. But he did not want to spoil my birthday. He wanted me to feel at ease in New York.

November was spent determining whether Kishan could be a candidate for a heart transplant. He really wanted to be. I was still in New York. I messaged him that I was reading the paper about the transplant. My parents were permitted to remain on site in Newcastle but not in Kish's hospital room overnight. Kish couldn't sleep so I took over the night duty. Virtually of course. I believe the document was 115 pages long.

He was afraid that the details of the transplant would frighten me. They did. He said that if I was frightened he wouldn't be able to sleep. Perhaps that's why he sent me home the day before he passed. He didn't want me to be scared of losing him.

He was not strong enough for the transplant: *Kish was admitted for urgent transplant assessment in context of suspicion of HCC against background of Fontan with failing physiology. At the moment Kish is not suitable for transplant due to severe frailty following local admission over Summertime with sepsis.*

This deepened his depression. A few weeks later, he chose to keep our closest cousins up to date on his health. His message read: *Hi everyone, I thought I should tell you all now but my health isn't great. My heart operation that I had when I was 6 isn't working as well now and my heart is failing. This is the reason for the fluid and recent illnesses etc. I have also been diagnosed with suspected liver cancer which is related to the heart failure. This is why I was recommended for a transplant and was in Newcastle hospital recently but that's not going to happen right now as I am too weak to deal with the recovery. Right now they can only optimize me with medication and Newcastle will do a heart catheter soon to see if they can make any internal changes but this will likely be after the cancer treatment. I'm in good spirits though as always.*

A bit of each of us broke inside. He had to be very brave to do this. Again I was not there to comfort him.

People tell me I shouldn't feel guilty. They tell me that Kish was so happy that I was fulfilling my dream. But they have no right to say that. They had no idea how much I hated every moment I was apart from him. Nobody can convince me I shouldn't live with the regret of missing out on the last six months of his life. No one can make that claim. I really should have gone back home.

The separation strained our relationship, especially when I went home for the holidays. I felt so disconnected from him. Consider this pain: your ailing brother feels uncomfortable in your presence.

We had to reconnect. We would have less than a month. We did make up for lost time during the holidays. But how was I meant to know I'd be losing my brother a month later. That remorse haunts me.

But then I remind myself that he waited for me to come home.

He allowed me to massage his legs again like I did during the summer. They were so thin. I was often scared a bone would break. That any pressure applied would make him feel even more pain. He was so fragile. But on December 15th I received the best news from Kishan. He didn't text much. He wasn't very social. Until this message. "Guys I made it." Followed by a selfie of him in his newly decorated bedroom. He had walked up the stairs for the first time in eight months. And then he did it a few more times. I thought he was getting stronger.

I have had to find Kish's bed many times before in the hospital. On that Thursday I was searching more urgently. I did not ask for directions. I dodged medical trolleys and swerved past medical waste bins. Strange looking equipment obstructed my path to his bed.

Kishan was usually in a side room when he had an infection. But the ward was congested so he was on an aisle bed without privacy. That absence of privacy always bothered me.

He didn't appear to be in good health. But at this moment I still had hope that he would pull through. He was having a lot more trouble breathing. His upper body appeared to rise higher with each breath. Kishan didn't appear upset. He might have been perplexed, but his mood was not too bad. Certainly not down.

Kish and I had only a fleeting encounter as the nurses were checking him. I left the ward with my dad. I bought a chocolate muffin. We both got coffee. We sat.

Dad was anxious. He was eerily silent. We didn't talk a whole lot. He would scroll through his phone to pass the time. I presume this was to inform our extended family of Kish's condition. His stats began to decline shortly after we left the ward. My mum hurried back out of the ward to summon us in. She was shaking.

My triplet cousins – our closest relatives – were traveling from

London. We call ourselves the *Famous Six*: Kishan, Dilan, Mansi, Krishan, Kajol and Karishma. The three of us and the three of them. When Kishan was ill he sought out Krishan in particular. They shared a passion for Arsenal. Immaculate banter between the two.

My mum said she and my dad would handle everything and sent me home to my grandma. Dilan was returning on the train from Manchester. There were many delays. I didn't know what to say to my grandma. We just waited for my cousins to arrive.

My memory of what I did before returning to the hospital that evening is hazy. I recall having a Zoom call about one of my classes. The triplets arrived and bought food. None of us had an appetite.

Kishan's oxygen levels had plummeted. My mum called Krishan to notify us. Ravi, my second cousin in London, and Riya, his sister in Birmingham also called me. I told them to get to the hospital as quickly as possible. I called Dilan, who was still encountering train delays. Fortunately, his girlfriend's dad was going to pick him up from the train station and drive him to the hospital. The triplets' mum and their brother-in-law were also coming from London.

I recall my grandma sobbing. It was as though she was forgetting to breathe. She was sitting and shaking as my mum explained the situation over the phone. But there was still hope at this stage. My mum then told us all to hurry to the hospital.

We left in two cars. I prefer to think of myself as a safe driver. But it was rush hour. I was driving recklessly, occasionally slipping into road rage. I *forgot* to pay for a parking ticket again and went straight to the ward.

I recall seeing several of our relatives already there. I took my grandma and my cousin Krishan in to see Kish. He was still trying to talk to us. "Don't cry," he said. "I'm fine."

Dilan finally arrived. I believe he sensed what was going to happen. "I thought he'd be okay and he'd be home in a few days," he later told me. "And Dad did tell me like, 'try come home, try come home, try come home'. But I kept saying I'm planning to come home on the weekend anyway."

Dilan wanted to be informed immediately what was going on. He had been worried on the train from Manchester. Kish was keeping

Mum and Dad busy. I was preoccupied with everyone else. Nobody was telling Dilan the truth about what was unfolding. So he texted Anuj, a close family friend. Anuj is a junior doctor and was working at the hospital.

"I messaged him, like, 'can you just tell me straight? What's going on? How bad is it?'" he says. "And he told me that it wasn't looking good, and that his lungs were really blocked up."

Dilan left Kishs' side and I followed him outside. It was the first time he had seen Kish in a week. We sobbed together. "I remember holding his hand," he says. "And he told me off because my hand was too hot."

Kishan was looking forward to seeing his best friends. He had known them since he was a child. He was eager to see all of his cousins. It was as if he was preparing everyone.

The hours blended together. I would stroke Kish's hand. We would listen to the Hanuman Chalisa, a Hindu devotional hymn. He would listen to the prayers every night for months on end. Hanuman kept him calm.

Dilan assumed the role of sending a few people at a time into Kish's room. It was the sort of role Kish always played. Our cousin Ravi assumed everyone was hungry so brought back nuggets, fries, and jalapeño poppers from Burger King. Dilan ate for both of us. He would often eat for the two of us.

People kept asking me "Are you okay?" "Do you require anything?" "Did you drink any water?"

No, no and no.

In a side room the nurses, the cardiology team, the doctors from intensive care and critical care, my mum, my dad and Anuj all congregated. I stayed with Kish. I sponged his mouth which the oxygen mask had dried.

When people came into the room Kish asked them if they'd eaten, or if there was a lot of traffic on the way to the hospital. His friends fist bumped him and talked about Arsenal. He reminded one friend of the bet they had made. Another FaceTimed from a business trip in America, telling Kish about an NBA game he'd seen. Kish hoped to attend an NBA game, too.

He kept asking about the meeting in the side room. He was terrified even if he would not admit it.

The doctor arrived. Kishan was impatient. He only wanted the truth. The doctor told him that his vital signs were deteriorating and advised him to try the BiPAP to help him breathe.

This was the last measure doctors could try. "Oh no," Kish said, "but we have to try it."

Dilan felt as though he could not bear to watch Kishan put on the mask and so stepped out of the room for that moment.

Kish tried it. It was painful to witness. His entire torso would lift with each breath. He was clearly distressed. He hated it. It looked like a gas mask from the war. Kishan was upset that he couldn't wear his glasses. He had the mask removed and replaced it with nasal cannulas.

Later, we came to believe that this was his moment of acceptance. He had fought long and hard enough.

We were all asked to leave while the nurses cleaned Kishan up to make him comfortable. I left the ward where everyone was gathered. My cousin Ravi tried again with the Burger King. I opted for a MisFit bar instead. And then I remembered to cancel my flight to New York.

Kishan was transferred to a private room. I see why.

I returned and lingered at his side. I rubbed his hand for hours. I moved to the side chair, wrapped myself with our favorite gray blanket, and cuddled his Arsenal pillow.

My plan was to stay the night. Kishan, on the other hand, had other plans for me. "Go home and rest," he said. He only wanted my parents to spend the night.

Maybe he would have asked me to stay if I had been present these past six months. Maybe he would have felt closer to me and wanted my company. But then I remember that only a week earlier when he was still home I was upstairs in my bedroom, packing. He told my mum, "tell Mansi to come downstairs." I was taken aback.

Kishan and I were never particularly cuddly. He disliked being fussed over or hugged. But he wished to be that evening. He wanted a hug from me.

At the hospital my relatives had slipped away a few hours earlier

LETTING KISHAN GO 119

to take my grandma home. Dilan and I left around midnight. I had a slice of pizza and went up to bed. Pizza was Kish's favorite. I didn't sleep through the night.

He had two last visitors at one in the morning. My cousin Raj and our uncle. They arrived from London. Kish was awake when they came. They spoke for five minutes. Kish couldn't understand everything they were saying. Kish's mouth was dry and he asked for a Fanta.

My mum and I had been exchanging messages since the early hours of the morning. Kish fell in and out of sleep. He kept asking my dad about his stats. My dad would say they were fine. But Kish could see the numbers in the reflection of the mirror.

He drank a lot of Fanta and Coca-Cola through the sponge my mum brought to his mouth.

At 4 in the morning he said, "Dad, I'm tired now." He fell asleep.

I texted my mum at 7 to ask whether everything was well. She replied that nothing had changed. He was sleeping. She sent me a list.

Dads glasses

Dads meds in kitchen cupboard brown basket

Dad a top/ socks

Toothbrush toothpaste

Me a top

I have leggings on anything to go with that

I woke Dilan. I put on any clothes I could find. I had grabbed my clothes that I had set out for the airport. It was just before 8. We told our cousins that we were leaving. We had no idea they would be required 15 minutes later.

We hurried to the hospital and entered the ward. I was perplexed when I saw Anuj the doctor in the waiting area with tears in his eyes. I rushed into Kish's room. My mum's closest friends were already there. Kishan was sleeping. I hadn't seen him sleep that soundly in a long time.

My mum and dad were standing next to Dilan and I. And I never uttered the word goodbye. I wanted to hear his voice one last time.

One by one people came into the room to say goodbye. It became extremely stuffy.

There must have been more than 40 of us. I don't remember

everyone who was there. The nurses lectured us for obstructing the corridor.

I took Kish's hand in mine and sat down on the bed. Hanuman Chalisa was playing. I do not know whether five minutes passed or an hour.

With the sponge, I gave him Coca-Cola one last time. He opened his eyes. He looked at me.

But all eyes were drawn to my mum. He had squeezed her hand. It was 1:42pm.

My grandma touched his chest. His heart had stopped.

In loving memory of Kishan Shayam Vithlani. 23rd January 1996 – 13th January 2023

TO FIND A
MOCKING BIRD

Alessia Alessandra Ling de Borbon

On Christmas morning in 1956, Nelle Harper Lee woke up in her friends' apartment in Manhattan and looked under the tree. She longed for her hometown in Alabama, but couldn't make it to her annual holiday visit because she needed to show up for work or risk losing her job. So the Browns decided to take her in for the holidays rather than leave her alone in her small, cold apartment.

That morning, Joy Brown told her to look under the Christmas tree. Lee saw a small white envelope bearing her name. She picked it up, opened it and saw that inside was a check. The amount represented a year's salary. Joy Brown told her that with this money, Lee could quit her job as an airline reservations agent. Now, Brown explained,

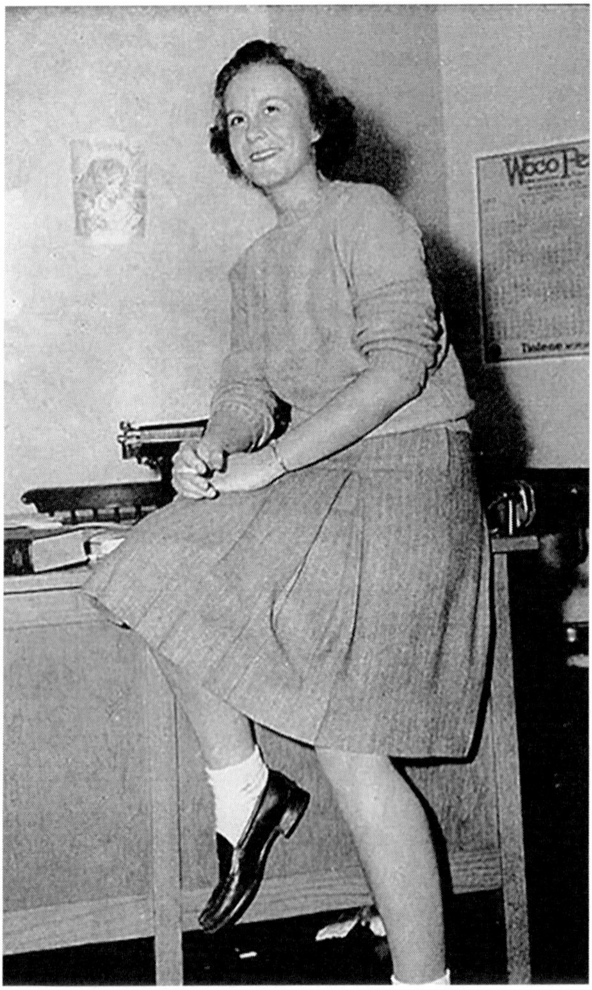

she was free to do what she had come to New York dreaming of doing: write.

But Lee was not relieved. She was terrified.

I had gone in search of Harper Lee, but not the author of *To Kill a Mockingbird*. I needed to know who she was before. Lee had not set out to become a writer. She was going to become a lawyer because that's what her father wanted. To be a writer meant to defy him. And that would mean taking a risk unlike any other she had ever faced.

I understood something about the terror she felt that Christmas morning – the fear that, given the chance to do what she had always hoped to do, she could fail. I also understood what it meant to do something other than what was expected.

How, I wondered, did Nelle Harper Lee do it?

She was 19 years old when, in the fall of 1945, she began to study law as an undergraduate at the University of Alabama. The campus at Tuscaloosa was 130 miles from her home in Monroeville, a town of less than 800 people. In this small city, few were more respected than her father.

Amasa Coleman Lee, known as A.C. but called Coley by his family, had grown up poor and devoutly Christian 50 miles away in Butler County. He was one of nine children. He worked a variety of jobs until he met his wife, Francis Cunningham Finch, at church. They married in 1910, and two years later A.C. Lee became financial manager for the law firm of Barnett & Bugg in Monroeville. In 1915, he passed the bar exam. The law firm changed its name to Barnett, Bugg & Lee.

He would later buy the local newspaper, the *Monroe Journal*, and appoint himself editor, a post he held for 18 years. He was also the local representative to the Alabama legislature. But it was his legal practice that would one day immortalize him, though in fictional form, as the inspiration for Atticus Finch, the lawyer who defends a wrongly accused Black man in his daughter's novel. The inspiration was based in fact: A.C. Lee did defend two black men, a father and son, accused of murdering a white man. He lost the case. The men were hanged.

Nelle Harper Lee did not connect with her mother, her biographer, Charles J. Shields, told me. But she adored and admired her father. Her father was an intellectual, "a man of ideas, he read, he debated, he was thoughtful."

A.C. Lee, in turn, saw potential in his daughter. He wanted her, Shields said, "to follow his footsteps and practice law in Alabama." So she did.

It did not go well. Lee was an outcast on campus. Shields recalled his interviews with Lee's classmates. They all said that, as intelligent and thoughtful as she was, she did not perform well in law school. "One of her classmates said flatly that she couldn't imagine Miss Lee being an attorney," he said. "She didn't have the drive."

Lee's father took notice. Her older sister, Alice, had graduated with a law degree from the same university in 1943 and was working for her father. Nelle, on the other hand, had been interested in literature since high school. Perhaps, he reasoned, she needed to get that out of her system.

So he offered his daughter a gift: a summer studying English literature at Oxford University. This way she would see that becoming an attorney would finance what he regarded as her hobby – traveling and writing.

She spent the summer of 1948 in England. And when she came back she told her family that she would be dropping out of law school. She was six months shy of graduating. Her best friend and childhood neighbor, Truman Capote, was telling her she should join him in New York.

She took a job as a waitress at the Monroeville golf club to save enough money to leave. Her father told her she did not have to become a lawyer but she should at least get her degree. He told her that staying would be a service not only to her family but to her community. But a year after dropping out of law school, she boarded a bus to New York. She was 23.

Leaving, said Charles J. Shields, "was a matter of perseverance and being in the right environment. Whether it was conducive to writers, if she could tell a Southern story, and she had plenty of Southern stories she wanted to tell. I think she once said that her ambition was to become sort of the Jane Austen of her part of the country."

As for the leaving itself, "Nelle considered the day she caught a train to New York City one of the happiest in her life," wrote Wayne Flynt, author of *Afternoons with Harper Lee*. "She never expressed regrets about leaving her family, law school, or Alabama."

But the pull home did not evaporate. In 1951 her mother and older brother Edwin died within six weeks of each other. Her mother had been sick for some time and her brother died of a cerebral hemorrhage while serving in the army. She returned for their funerals. Then she went back to New York.

She arrived in New York with little money and no assurance that her plan to become a writer in New York would succeed. She moved into a shoddy, cold-water apartment at 1539 York Avenue and frequented a bar on 79th Street. For six years, she worked as a clerk for British Overseas Airways Corporation. She wrote at night and on weekends. Nothing she wrote was published.

She had no interest in becoming a part of Capote's literary world – going to expensive restaurants and mingling with high-society friends. But it was through that in 1954, five years after leaving home, that she met the Browns. Michael was a composer and lyricist. Joy had once been a ballet dancer. Lee became a frequent guest at their townhouse on East 50th Street, a 10-minute subway ride but a world away from her apartment.

Michael Brown introduced her to his agents Annie Laurie Williams and her husband Maurice Crain. They were Southerners who had for a time represented Capote, whom they found "difficult." Lee showed them her stories. They told her that while she was a talented storyteller, short stories were a tougher sell than novels.

Lee was intimidated by the advice. She had already spent over six years working on these short stories, but decided to follow it and began working on a novel, *Go Set a Watchman*, that would not be published for another 60 years. Still, making time to write was difficult. She was now 30, unpublished and unsure whether she ever would be.

That December came the Christmas gift from the Browns.

The one stern string attached is that I will be subjected to a sort of 19th Century regimen of discipline: they don't care whether anything I write makes a nickel," she wrote to a friend back home. "They want to lick me into some kind of seriousness toward my talents, which of course will destroy anything amiable in my character, but will set me on the road to a career of sorts … Aside from the etceteras of gratefulness and astonishment I feel about this proposition, I have a horrible feeling that this will be the making of me, that it will be goodbye to the joys of messing about. So for the coming year I have laid in 3 pairs of Bermuda shorts, since I shall rarely emerge from 1539 York Avenue.

My parents both studied engineering. My mother became a doctor, and when I was young she would make gifts for me of stethoscopes and heart models. My parents never said directly that they wanted me to become an engineer but the messages were clear.

I tried to like engineering. In fact, that was my undergraduate major. But in my senior year, having completed my required coursework, I had some additional credits I could use however I wanted. I enrolled in classes on American Fiction After World War Two and the American Short Story. I took a basic journalism class, too.

My parents wanted me to go to graduate school. My father hoped I would go to business school and my mother wanted me to go to medical school. I told them I was thinking of English or journalism. My mother was concerned.

My father, drawing unintentionally on A.C. Lee's approach, suggested I try journalism school. But with a caveat: when I was done I could go to business school. As it happened he had wanted me to skip grades in school so that I might have a few years after college to "make mistakes."

I do not know whether A.C. Lee thought his daughter made a mistake when she moved to New York. He died in 1962, two years after the publication of *To Kill a Mockingbird*.

MY MOTHER'S CURSE

McKenna Nicole Leavens

Please be advised that this story contains descriptions of child sexual abuse.

She was six years old. Her mother left her alone sitting on his lap as she went to fetch her brother from the school bus. He slipped his hand down her pants. She flinched. He whispered, don't tell anyone. So she didn't. She said nothing then or the next time or all the times in all the years that followed. Now she was 23 and she was a beauty queen with the crown and the sash to prove it. She had come to South Padre, Texas to compete to become Miss USA. She was there with her best friend, Matt, her mother and her abuser. She believed she had a chance.

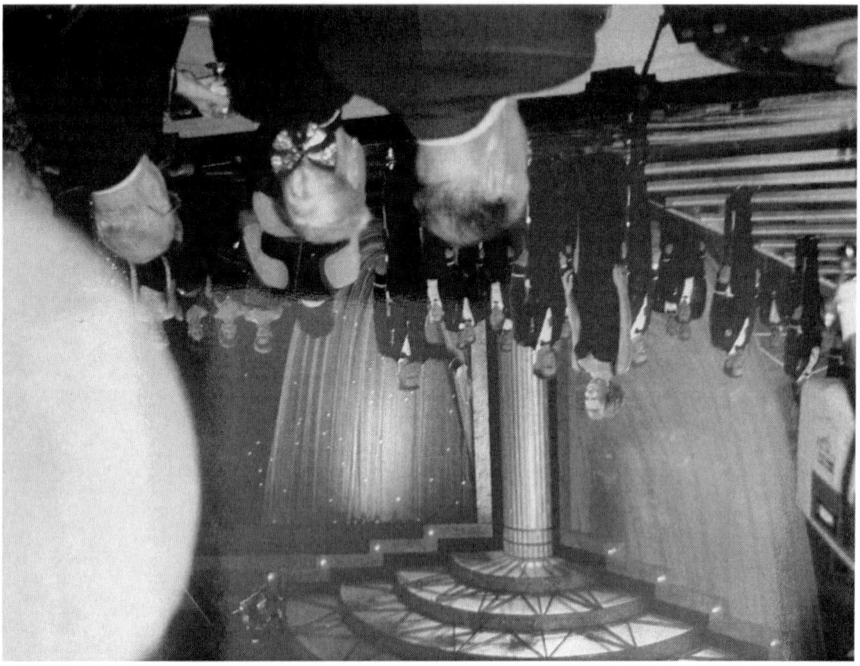

Her name is Shara. She is my mother.

She had been preparing for this pageant all her life. She took dance lessons, acting lessons, and when she was a child her mother began entering her in beauty pageants. Now she was Miss Arizona. If she won the Miss USA pageant her future could be one of great possibilities. She might even become a star.

She arrived in South Padre ten days before the show and for those ten days she rehearsed, worked out twice a day, and stayed on a strict diet.

When it was over her mother and her friend were waiting for her, along with Fred, her mother's husband and her abuser. They were waiting for her in the lobby and when she saw them she began to cry.

My grandparents divorced when my mother was five years old. Shortly afterwards my grandmother got together with Fred, with whom she had been having an affair. They moved three hours away from my mother's home in Morenci, AZ to Tucson so they could go be with Fred. He insisted that my mother call him "Pa." The three of them lived in a small apartment in the middle of town– while her brother, Korey, traveled back and forth between their house and their dad's home in Morenci.

My grandmother often took my mom to stay in hotels. She told her it was to take a vacation. But really it was to escape Pa. My mom had watched him yell and throw things at my grandmother. He would always find us, she told me, no matter how far away we ran.

He wouldn't touch her again until she started the first grade. The three of them would lay down in the afternoons for a nap after my mom got home from school. She would lay next to her mom who was curled up next to Pa on the other side of the bed. When her mother was facing away he would reach over and touch her. This happened for about a year. My mom finally decided to say something. She was almost eight. She mustered up the words to tell her mother, who replied, sweetie, you must've pushed his hand down there and he showed you what boys shouldn't do.

She set out alone for South Padre. All 51 girls were expected to arrive early to rehearse every day and do media appearances. There was an opening dance number that was my mom's dream because she was one of the few contestants who was also a dancer. The choreographer put her front and center. During rehearsals he would tell everyone to watch Shara because she knew what she was doing. She was excited that her best friend Matt would be coming to watch her.

Years later, my mother wrote, *"I remember the first time I saw him, Matt. Standing in a long line of eager uppies all waiting for a turn to show our performance abilities. It was the summer of 1989, week two of staging."*

My mom met Matt through her time at *Up With People*, a nonprofit that sent singers and dancers to perform around the world. He was a singer and she was a dancer. *"As I stood in that line, I felt timid and insecure, still conscious of the extra pounds I could never seem to take off, and questioning my worth and talent."*

She was 18 and in love with Matt. They spent two years together on the road in *Up With People* and she pursued him the entire time. One day he looked at her and said, Shara I'm gay. They remained inseparable. He encouraged her to compete in the Miss Arizona pageant and after she won, he encouraged her to be a judge for Miss Gay Arizona. Her mother and Pa did not want her involved in a contest for gay people because they thought it would damage the image they had worked so hard to build. She moved out of their house to live with Matt. They hated him.

Years later she wrote, *"It is a certainty that negative events will impact everyone's life and it is also certain that positive ones will as well. What we do with these events defines our life, our joy, our growth. This much I know to be absolutely one hundred percent, the truth."*

They left Tucson in the summer between my mom's second and third years of school. Pa and my grandmother moved my mom and Korey to Nogales, AZ, to a little town called Pena Blanca. They bought a lake resort. They fished and swam every weekend. My mom spent a lot of time by herself that summer. She didn't have a lot of friends and she liked that. She had no one she needed to impress or entertain.

She could lose herself in a fantasy world of being safe, beautiful and thin. They owned and managed the restaurant and boat dock as well as a small six-until motel. They lived in a trailer behind the restaurant. It was small but big enough for my mom to have her own room. Pa could be alone with her to do what he pleased. He would sneak into her room in the mornings while she was sleeping.

She later wrote of Pa, *"to this day I still get the 'icky' feeling when he tries to embrace myself or my daughters."*

One weekend the four of them drove to a resort in Rio Rico, AZ to spend some time by the pool and take a break from Pena Blanca. Something set Pa off and my mom remembers looking over to see her mother screaming as he pinned her against the wall and held a knife to her throat. Korey was ten years old and my mother was eight. She ran to the balcony and screamed, "He's going to kill her, please help us, he's going to kill her."

She believed she saved her mother's life.

The pageant was two days away. For eight days the contestants would wake up, work out, eat, rehearse and talk to the media. Now the competition was about to begin and my mother was ready for the preliminary judging.

It began on a Wednesday with swimsuits and evening gowns. On Thursday they would do the interviews and though the events were not televised, friends and relatives could watch. Her mother was there with Pa. Matt was there, too.

On Wednesday night my mother was backstage and like the other contestants was having her hair and makeup done. She never let anyone touch her hair because she knew exactly how she wanted it. She wore it down, curly and with a lot of volume. But tonight was different. Tonight she would let a hairdresser put her hair up in a bun. She also had another important decision to make: her gown. She was unsure. Her mother and Pa wanted her in a bright color, something poofy that would make her stand out. But Matt told her to go with something simple because her own beauty would speak for itself. So that's what she did.

When her name was called she walked out in a slim fitting black evening gown. This was the first time she had disobeyed her mother and Pa. Matt was proud of her.

The four of them left Pena Blanca when my mom started fourth grade. They moved to Wyoming where Pa got a job on the oil rig. He didn't bother my mom in Wyoming. She was ten and maturing quickly. She was ever more aware of what he was doing to her and how he acted around other girls her age. She remembers him looking at other young girls the way he looked at her. She remembers him making sexual jokes. The "icky" feeling stayed with her.

The following year they moved back to Arizona to a place called Oracle. She was excited because they were closer to her father who was only a 45 minute drive away. She thought his presence would protect her. She was wrong.

One night my mother had a friend over for a sleepover. In the morning she woke with Pa touching her breasts. She was shocked that he would risk being caught with her friend sleeping next to her. She wrote, *"Every time he entered the room my nervous system would scream danger, and yet the adults in my life were calm. How could this be? How could no one else see and feel what I did?"*

In the mornings he would go into her room and touch her. She would pretend to be asleep. And when he was done he would leave money on her dresser. Sometimes it would be a few dollars but other times it would be only a couple of cents.

My mom started to get her period. That didn't stop the abuse. It just wasn't as frequent because she tried to stay away from home. But as she looked more and more like a woman Pa lost interest. Sometimes she believed he had finally stopped. But then she'd be woken up in the mornings to a touch and some money left on her bedside table. His scent always woke her. She would remember it as a mix of cologne and sweat. She wrote, *"I always heard him, always felt his presence."*

She was approaching 13 the last time it happened. She had a boyfriend. She was becoming independent and spoke her mind. That morning he shuffled into her room as she pretended to be asleep. He invaded her. He left money on the counter and shuffled out. But this time she got out of bed and ran into her mother's room where she was

134   MY MOTHER'S CURSE

laying in bed and where Pa had returned. She looked at her and said, "If he ever lays a fucking hand on me again I will kill him."

Her mother said, "What are you talking about honey?"

Miss USA 1995 was crowned before a live television audience on February 10th, a Friday. My mother had spent the day preparing. This time she did her own hair, just as she always had. And as the telecast neared, she was backstage rehearsing for the big dance number, her signature moment.

The telecast began at 8 o'clock on the east coast with my mother at center stage. As she danced, she spotted Matt beaming at her. She had never felt more confident and reassured than to see him sitting in the audience. Her mother and Pa were out there, somewhere.

All the girls lined up alphabetically, according to the name of their state. They all wore the same outfit – a red bikini top and a red silk skirt to match. Then they waited to hear who among them had made the final 12. My mom held hands with the girls next to her.

"Miss Kentucky, Miss Missouri, Miss Maryland, Miss Massachusetts, Miss Illinois, Miss Florida, Miss New York, Miss Oklahoma, Miss Rhode Island, Miss Minnesota, Miss Louisiana and Miss Texas…,"

She snuck out the side door. She took out the pack of American Spirit cigarettes she'd been hiding all week. She would have to wait until the show was over because they would call out all the contestants for the finale. She had to keep her Miss Arizona sash on, which now smelled of cigarette smoke. She said to herself, "I'm still a beauty queen. I'm still a beauty queen."

She swore to herself she was not going to cry. But as soon as she stepped into the lobby she saw Matt and the tears came. Matt hugged her. She looked at her mother and Pa.

Your hair was wrong and you chose the wrong dress, they said, and then they turned to leave.

AN UNEXPECTED FRIENDSHIP IN TIMES OF WAR

Maria Sole Campinoti

Like so many great human stories, the one of Vittorio Cugnach happened by chance. What led him to risk his life and that of his family to bring Laura Nunes Vais, Federico Weil, and five Jewish relatives from the Tuscan countryside to neutral Switzerland during the Holocaust was not planned. It happened due to a mix of events, emotions and untangled twists of fate.

By an almost unfathomable coincidence that unites people in some sort of divine order, I grew up in the house where this story takes place. I walked the same hallways, danced in the same rooms, and climbed the same oaks in the garden as did the characters of this

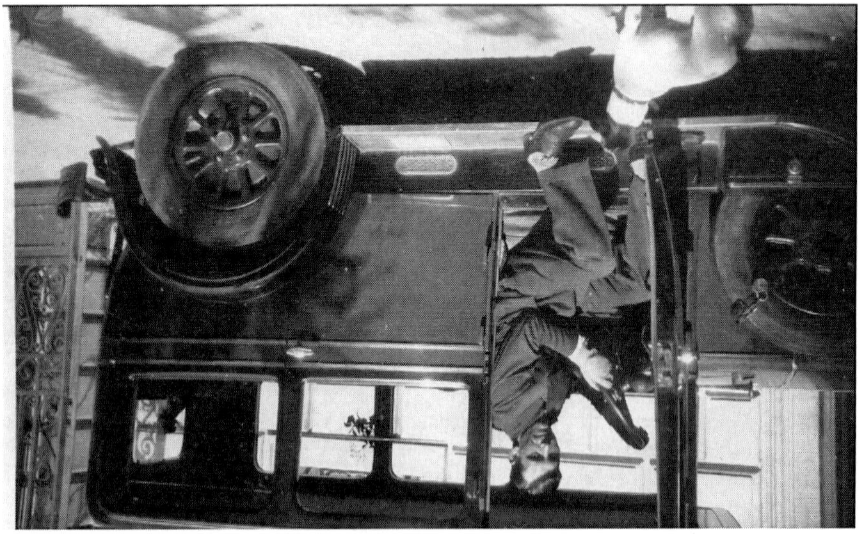

tale.

To understand what makes ordinary people perform extraordinary acts, it is necessary to rewind and tell the story of the unlikely friendship between Vittorio Cugnach and Federico Weil.

Vittorio Cugnach was born in Germany in 1903 to an Italian family who migrated from the northern town of Sala in the province of Belluno. His father worked building roads and moved to Germany hoping to make a fortune. Vittorio attended school in Germany until 1914, when all Italian families were encouraged to repatriate at the start of World War One. Anna Cugnach, Vittorio's daughter, remembers how back in Italy his classmates would call him "the German." He hated the nickname.

After the war Vittorio did his compulsory military service. Then he needed to find a job. That is when he chanced upon Federico Weil, a man 20 years his senior who owned a steel factory in Milan. Weil hired him to work in the warehouse.

Vittorio, however, was destined for more. He impressed Federico Weil, who offered him a job as his chauffeur. The job came with a house and a good salary. Vittorio needed a driver's license and when he got one the course of his life and Weil's began to change.

Vittorio drove Weil across Italy on business and leisure trips, especially between Milan and Genova, where Federico had business and family. As they drove together they struck up an unlikely friendship, given their differences in income and social standing. Vittorio was loyal, intelligent and ingenious. If the car broke down, his daughter says, he always knew how to fix it.

It was in the port city of Livorno where Weil met the love of his life – Laura Nunes Vais, the only daughter of Mario Nunes Vais and Sofia Eloise Uzzielli, who came from a distinguished Florentine family. The couple was initially timid with one another, but in time fell in love and married. Federico, and consequently, Vittorio, spent more time at Villa Nunes Vais, Laura's parents' country estate near Florence.

There were many parties and many celebrated guests at the villa – writers, poets, artists, composers and politicians, too. Laura and

Federico would one day become famous hosts, as well, and made no distinctions between the social classes in whom they invited into their home.

The villa was situated outside the city's walls in what was then the countryside. It was set amongst the rolling hills dotted with medieval and Renaissance villas. It had remained unchanged for centuries.

It was at the villa that Vittorio met his wife, Ida Bartolozzi. Her family had long been the Nunes Vais' farmers and gardeners and lived in the farmhouse across from the villa. Ida was born in the farmhouse, and as a young girl, in fact, had witnessed the birth of Laura Nunes Vais. Marrying Ida connected Vittorio to the villa and to the Weil family forever. He and Ida would have three children – Franco, Anna, and Carlo – who grew alongside the villa.

In the early years of their marriage, Laura and Federico lived in Genova. Vittorio spent many days and weeks away from his family, driving Federico. In their absence, a bond developed between Ida and Laura. It was Laura who helped Ida when she gave birth to her second child, Anna, in 1936.

Those years were also marked by the rise of Fascism and life became ever more imperiled for Italy's Jews. The newly enacted Racial laws banned Jewish people from attending and teaching in non-Jewish schools, from working for the government as well as for banks and insurance companies. They could not marry people of the "Aryan race," nor could they care for an "Aryan child." Many Jews were stripped of their property and barred for working as journalists, notaries, doctors and veterinarians.

So it was that in 1942, after the outbreak of World War Two, the Weils fled Genova for what they hoped would be the safety of Villa Nunes Vais.

Vittorio Cugnach, says his daughter Anna, never supported Fascism and Mussolini, not even in its early days. Yet he never directly opposed it. She remembers her older brother Franco dressed up for school as a *balilla* with black pants, a black jacket, and a scarf with the colors of the Italian flag in honor of the Fascist paramilitary youth movement, which was required of every child.

Vittorio continued living with his family at the villa even though he could no longer officially be an employee of the Weils. Meanwhile, life in the villa proceeded much as it always had. Laura and Federico continued to host parties and gathered with their friends and relatives.

Laura and Federico had no children of their own, and so extended their affection to local children. On summer afternoons children were invited into the garden, where they played croquet and at night adults were invited to gather in the garden to gaze at the stars and trade stories.

Laura was especially fond of the children of Ida and Vittorio. She and Federico paid their school fees. Laura gave them clothing her niece no longer wore.

When Mussolini's regime collapsed in July of 1943, Italian Jews were cautiously happy. But the happiness was short-lived because in September, Hitler established a puppet government in Italy, once again under the rule of Mussolini, and the Jewish population fell into despair. The mass deportations to the death camps were about to begin. On October 16, 1943, German police stormed the Jewish ghetto in Rome and deported more than 1000 people, most of them to Auschwitz. Villa Nunes Vais was no longer a haven. The Weils knew they had little time to escape. They turned to Vittorio.

The plan was anything but simple. In addition to Federico and Laura, the Weils also had five relatives who had managed to escape from Rome to the villa. Everyone would have to be moved and quickly. Vittorio had relatives living south of Florence who might hide them.

That is where he first brought them. But it soon became clear they could not all stay. They would have to be separated. He drove Federico and Laura to the home of an opera singer whose musical studies Laura had subsidized. He brought the two youngest relatives from Rome to the home of his cousin and left the other three with his relatives outside of Florence.

During the weeks when everyone was in their hideouts, Vittorio traveled between the safe houses to bring news about the others.

But even the plan began to fall apart as the roundups grew closer.

So Vittorio collected everyone and brought them all to the home of the opera singer's mother. Years later the two youngest relatives would remember walking many hours with Vittorio along country trails from one hideout to the other. The most frightening moment came when they were crossing the Arno, the river that flows through Florence. German commandos were constantly on the lookout for Jewish families trying to flee the city. Together with Vittorio they found a boatman to ferry them across the riverbank at dusk. But to keep silent the boatman did not dip his oars into the water and instead pulled them across with a rope that extended to both sides of the river.

The reunion with the rest of the group would have to be brief. Italy was becoming too dangerous. It was time to chance crossing the border – a risk for them all, including Vittorio.

It was now December. Vittorio would not tell Ida where he was going when he disappeared with the Weils and their relatives. In fact, they had made their way to Florence where one night they all boarded a train to Milan. The group split up to avoid suspicion. Vittorio made believe the two youngest children were his. Four times that night the train stopped during air raids and each time everyone had to get out, leaving them further exposed. Finally they arrived in Milan and there at the station they waited to board a train that would take them north, toward a village near Lake Como and the Swiss border.

At the village they met a band of smugglers who offered to lead them into Switzerland which was only a few hours walk away. Federico and Laura were the first to set out for the border. Vittorio joined them with the smugglers. German soldiers were patrolling the border which was marked by an iron fence. They would need to avoid the soldiers and somehow burrow under the fence.

The smugglers pointed to where they would find the closest village on the other side of the border. Vittorio went back for the others. The youngest would remember how her father stuffed a handkerchief in her mouth to keep her silent. They walked along winding paths. The wind made it bitter cold. The smugglers helped them carry their two suitcases. Finally, they crossed the border and found a house where they were invited inside. The youngest were given milk and sugar.

Swiss border authorities registered the entrance into the country of Federico, Laura and the others on February 2, 1944.

By the time he finally returned to Villa Nunes Vais, Vittorio had a raging fever. But he told his wife nothing about what he had done and where he had been. Only one Jewish relative was left behind – Giulia Weil, who was too old and sick to escape. She died shortly after. Vittorio secretly went to Florence to find a rabbi to bless her.

Florence was liberated in August of 1944. The war ended the following May and in September of 1945, the British troops who had occupied Villa Nunes Vais departed. The Weil returned to Italy. Their relatives returned to Rome. Laura and Federico resumed their lives, moving between Milan, Genova and Florence.

Villa Nunes Vais, meanwhile, was temporarily requisitioned by the Italian government to provide housing for families displaced during the war. Vittorio and his family lived in the ground floor apartment. Laura and Federico moved into the apartment with them when they returned to the villa.

In fact, Federico never fully reclaimed Villa Nunes Vais; he died of cancer in 1950 in Milan. On his deathbed Federico told Vittorio never to abandon Laura and to take care of her for the rest of her life.

Laura moved between her mother's family house in Florence and the villa. She rented out apartments, invited guests and hosted recitals to keep from being lonely. Vittorio spent more time with his family, taking walks along the country roads to church every Sunday.

Vittorio died in 1970, after suffering a second heart attack. Laura told his daughter Anna that after her husband the person that she missed the most was Vittorio. Ida and Laura were widows together and sought each other's company. In 2006 Vittorio was conferred the title of Righteous Amongst the Nations, a title given by the State of Israel to non-Jews who risked their lives to save Jews during the Holocaust.

Anna was now a young woman, but leaving Villa Nunes Vais had never crossed her mind; she had to care for Laura and Ida. She would accompany Laura at the theater and to run errands around town.

As Laura got older and more frail her vitality began to vanish and she became ever more fearful and gloomy. She often asked Anna and her husband to check for people hiding in the bushes.

Laura died in 1988. Her Roman relatives who had escaped with her and Federico, inherited the villa Laura's family had owned for 150 years. The relatives considered selling it, but only if Anna and Ida agreed.

They had spent so much of their lives there, but they asked themselves what purpose would there be in staying? To stay meant enduring a life of desolate loneliness and all the reminders of what the villa once was and could never be again.

So the year after Laura died Anna, her husband, and Ida left the villa. They moved two hours away to be closer to Anna's brothers. The villa was sold to a local bank and later to a real estate company that renovated it, dividing the villa into apartments. Among the buyers were my parents.

The apartment complex where I grew up is still called Villa Nunes Vais. From the outside it looks much as it did in the years when it belonged to Laura's family, and in the years when Vittorio, Ida and their children lived there. Despite the extensive renovations the interior is reminiscent of the past. The building has been designated a landmark and the architects had to maintain vestiges of the past. The garden remains the same and there is still a farmhouse.

Anna is now in her mid-90s and lives in a home for the elderly. Although she is quite frail, her memories of her life at the villa, of the Weils and of what her father did to save a family of Jews fleeing for their lives remains strong.

I asked Anna what it was like to leave Villa Nunes Vais, a home that, after all, was where she lived because her father was the chauffeur for the owners.

It was, she said, the end of our world.

A PORTRAIT OF MY IMPERFECT FATHER

Averee Nelson

In an unexpected turn of events, my brother Miles decided to stop working for my dad's hauling and demolition business and instead got a job at a local grocery store. Miles has been working with my dad on and off for the last eight years since he was in high school, and although it hasn't been easy for him at times (because of the manual labor), I didn't expect him to stop working for my dad right now.

As my dad gets older, the idea of him working alone, doing hard physical work, is scary. At least with my brother being there, my dad has someone to rely on. Now it feels like my dad is suddenly all alone again.

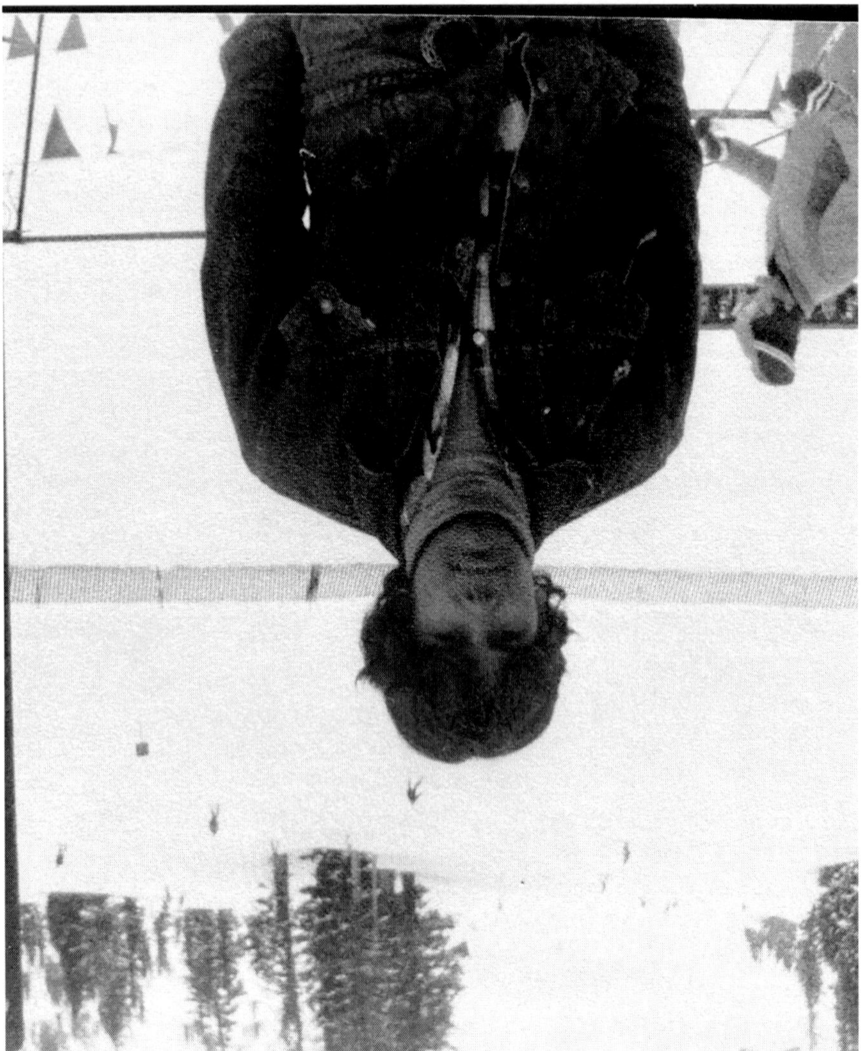

Miles has been my dad's right-hand man. My dad has taught Miles all the tricks of the trade. Between ripping out flooring, breaking down concrete and trips back and forth to the dump, they have spent a lot of time together on work days. My dad half-jokingly described his personality as a mix between silliness and anger, so a person could only imagine what it is like to work with him and live in his home.

I talked to my dad about Miles working at the grocery store rather than with him, and my dad pointed out that Miles is choosing the job that has fewer benefits. He kept going on about how he pays Miles more per hour than the grocery store and the other benefits of working with him. This is just another reminder that his kids won't be with him forever, but he also doesn't want us to feel held back in any way.

My sister, Tamra, joked that my dad's biggest dream is to have all of us living in his house forever. He doesn't want to be alone, but he also knows that we will all eventually move out and find our ways in life. My dad does not expect Miles and his boyfriend, Shaun, to live with him forever, but it is a sad reality he will have to face. It is so natural for my dad to have his kids relying on him and being around him, and when we are gone it will feel like a drastic change.

My dad told me about how Sundays used to be his least favorite day. I asked him why. He said it was because that was the day my mom would pick us up from his house because we always spent the weekends with him after they got divorced. He remembers the happy feeling of having us in the house every weekend, and then the silence after my mom picked us up Sunday evenings. He was sad to be alone, and this feeling taps into when he was a young boy. Back then he filled that loneliness with drugs. Now it is different.

I didn't tell Miles that I was a little sad that he was no longer working with our dad. Miles has no regrets about changing jobs.

"He doesn't want me to get a different job because he wants me to work for him," Miles told me. "He is probably worried about our relationship waning, if anything, me working with him less will make our relationship better."

Then he said, "He is going to have to accept the fact that me and Shaun are going to move away soon."

I ask him why they are thinking of moving out soon. They both are living rent-free and are being fed almost every night with the food my dad buys, and the list goes on. And my dad likes taking care of them. Miles is about to complete his undergraduate education with a history degree, and he plans on getting his teaching credential. It makes sense that he would live with my dad while going to school, especially since he was working with him. And they are still saving up to afford to move out. Miles said when they do move out, they will have to at least move a half hour inland from the coast in order to afford an apartment. Then he rambled on about capitalism and Marxist theory.

Miles then turned my questions back on me and said my relationship with our dad is contentious. I said I wouldn't put it like that. "You wouldn't say your relationship with dad is contentious?" he asked.

Miles said that every time I visit home I don't spend a lot of time making plans with our dad. It is true my dad gets a little upset that I don't spend every waking moment with him when I am home, but I feel like he is being melodramatic.

"In his mind, we have to go out of our way to do chores and invite him to things, and if we don't, then he will resent us for it," Miles said. But in our minds as his kids, "We think he needs to reach out and ask for help instead of expecting us to figure it out."

Miles said he wants us to have a "moral loyalty" towards our dad.

My dad doesn't usually ask for help. I wonder how he will be able to adapt this time, and whether he knows he will have to.

My dad, Brett Nelson, was born in Santa Monica in 1959 but grew up in Cardiff, a beach community in Encinitas, California. His family lived in a house a mile from the ocean, in an area surrounded by eucalyptus trees. He was the baby of the family with two older sisters. My dad likes to say he was the "chosen one." He was coddled by his mom and grandmother – "spoiled and pampered," said my aunt Rena.

Rena would dress him up in tutus and high heels. He got away with a lot. He always had a rebellious streak, even as a child. When he was three years old, he was in a car his father was working on in their driveway when my dad released the parking brake. The car rolled across the street and through the neighbor's fence. And at the age of five, he snuck away from home to join the circus. His parents did not always know what he was up to. His parents divorced when he was in the first grade. His father moved out and his life changed.

As a teenager he liked riding his skateboard, surfing and smoking weed. He remembers his mom planting a pine tree in front of the house that got so massive that he and his friends and kids they barely knew would hide between the branches and smoke weed and drink beer.

He smoked his first joint when he was 12 years old. He was 13, misbehaving in school and disobedient at home when his mother kicked him out of her house and sent him to live with his father in El Centro.

"I knew he was up to trouble, and I just didn't want to have any part of it," Rena said.

El Centro was a farm community two hours away and 12 miles from the Mexican border. He lived with his father, his stepmother and her kid. He was in the middle of nowhere and knew nobody.

He went to school and was mostly staying out of trouble except for smoking cigarettes. But when his sisters came to pick him up to visit his mother he'd return to El Centro with weed. He spent most days doing work on his father's farm, going to school and he even got a job at a local restaurant to prove himself to his father and to stay out of trouble. He saved up enough money to buy a motorcycle. But nothing he did was good enough to please his father and stepmother. Whenever he made a mistake, he was met with snide remarks from his stepmother and violence from his father.

One night when he got permission to drive his father's car to the restaurant, he accidentally drove into a ditch beside the parking lot. A friend from work called a tow truck and called my dad's father, too. His father was drunk when he arrived and ignored my dad's apologies for messing up once again. His father punched him to the ground.

And yet, it was his stepmother who made his life ultimately unbearable. My dad could forgive his own father for the abuse because he yearned for his validation. But he couldn't forgive or forget how he was treated by his stepmother. He felt undermined by her. Even in the smallest ways, she reminded him that was not really part of his father's new family – like putting Ding Dong snacks in her own child's lunch boxes but not his.

The boiling point came when my dad finally stood up to her and demanded to know why she treated him the way she did. The conversation ended with her forcing his father to choose between him and her. He chose her.

Not too long after, my dad moved back to Cardiff, dropped out of high school and started dealing drugs. He understood that if he was going to be on his own he needed money. When he made enough he moved out of his mother's home.

He was 17 when he was arrested for the first time.

A few months ago, my brother and his boyfriend decided to have an intervention of sorts with my dad. They wanted to address their problems and concerns. When my dad works long days by himself, he often comes home agitated. When he is in a good mood, he is usually out on dates. And in between work and dates, he is smoking cigarettes and brewing shots from his Nespresso machine.

Miles had told me that life for him and his boyfriend Shaun had become difficult living with dad. Working with our dad had pushed Miles over the edge, which is part of why he quit. So Miles sat dad down and laid it out. That he was dating too many women, working too hard and drinking too much coffee. And that he had stopped going to NA meetings. My concern for my dad was genuine.

Miles told me, "I think his lifestyle is unhealthy, and I told dad that his lifestyle is unhealthy." But it is how he deals with sobriety now.

"We all sat down with him and told him that he hasn't been to NA meetings in a long time and I said 'I think your lack of grounding is manifesting through overworking, hyper aggression, and seeking validation from women,'" Miles said.

My dad had stopped going to NA meetings during the pandemic. He joined the local meetings through Zoom for a while, but that routine wasn't the same as going in person. Ever since Miles and I were in high school, my dad started dating more and that was actually the first time we had seen him dating since being with my mom. My dad says that he didn't want us to see him dating when we were younger because he wanted us to have a steady routine at his house, without different women coming in and out of our lives. But now, that is a different story.

I asked Miles why he thinks our dad is the way he is. Miles replied saying that he is a "product of his nature and his nurture."

"Product of a fucked up bloodline if you look at his dad," he added.

To Miles, it seemed like the intervention was a breakthrough. But when I asked my dad he could hardly remember what they were upset about.

"He said something about having a hobby and doing stuff because I work and do this and that – I get it," dad said.

"Do you get it?" I asked.

"Yeah, I do," he replied. "That actually surprised me and it made me feel good that he thought that way. It didn't hurt my feelings at all. Initially, we started off kind of angry and then it ended up like we were hugging and telling each other 'I love you' because we thought it was good. It was constructive and what I took from the conversation was that it was heartfelt."

I brought up how Miles was worried that my dad hasn't been going to NA meetings. "I need to go back to meetings," he said. "I'm not going to never go to meetings again, that's for sure."

I asked him how he stays sober.

"Smoke cigarettes, drink coffee, and be grateful," he said.

But what about the women?

"I guess that's a distraction."

After my dad's first arrest, he spent the next two decades of his life in and out of jail and prison. The longest stretch was 16 months. This routine was grueling. He ended up in jail maybe eight or ten times, sometimes spending a day, 30 days, six to nine months, and once over a year.

He was around 30 the last time he was in jail, and it was only for one day. That would be the last time before he finally got sober.

He couldn't get out of the cycle of dealing drugs while also being addicted. He also did not care about himself or the people around him.

"By the time I was 17," he told me, "I was thinking about dealing drugs, so unless my parents could come up with a better plan where I could make a decent amount of money, more money than I was making or something comparable, I wasn't gonna listen to it. I already had my mind made up."

Once after he was released from jail his sister, Rena, let him move in with her. She had bought a two-bedroom condo for herself and thought it would be nice to offer him one of the bedrooms. Perhaps in the beginning, she thought this would be the opportunity for my dad to stop getting into trouble. But Rena was horrified when police came to her door in the middle of the night asking questions about my dad. She was even more horrified after she made my dad move out, and found that her condo had been broken into in the middle of the night by someone looking for my dad.

"I was trying to help him out, give him a place to stay, give him an opportunity to get a job, and get his life together," said Rena. "And because he was doing what he was doing, the drugs and stuff, you know, people who are doing drugs, they're not thinking about anybody but themselves."

"I was just enabling him, I wasn't really helping him."

But then he became a father and that changed everything.

"I always think what triggered him to finally stop the silliness and drugs, you know, moving on and getting clean and sober and all that – what finally clicked for him – you know, he says it was Tamra," Rena told me.

Still, it took years after she was born for him to finally seek help.

"I kept having this recurring thought at three in the morning when I was trying to go to sleep," my dad recalled: "How was I going to get her to kindergarten next year when I was going to sleep when everybody else was waking up?

"I couldn't figure out how I would get her to school when I was still getting high."

No one has ever said that sobriety is easy, and it felt like another alienating experience to my dad. He recalls feeling nervous reentering society sober because he hadn't been sober since he was a teenager. He didn't know what it was going to be like to live in Cardiff without drugs and connect with people without drugs being involved.

He started the Twelve-Step Program in NA and through it found equilibrium in his life. It felt good. He made good with the people he hurt.

"I remember him coming to me at one point asking basically for forgiveness for all the shitty things he did," Rena told me. "I think it's something about blood and family, like, if anybody else would have treated me that way, I don't know if I could have forgiven them. But, you know, there's something about blood and family that you gotta stick together – I mean, I want that connection."

In 1998, my dad met my mom in Oceanside. Miles was born the following year. They got married and had me. My dad bought a house and then bought another. His hauling and demolition business had been in the works since he got sober and his business was successful. Those were the golden years.

The marriage, however, ended after ten years, but he never went back to using. He didn't make it an option. He hasn't been able to find a lasting partner since. It's not like he hasn't been looking, but I'm not sure if it has been for the right reasons.

"I wish he could find someone," Rena said. "I think it would be really nice for him to find someone."

He's a "workaholic," she said, a tendency she has, too. His mind turns to work as soon as he wakes up and starts doing something. He will be talking on the phone while watching the news early in the morning after his first cup of coffee and first cigarette. Then he will make his lunch for the day, load his truck and make a shot or two of espresso before heading out. There is a high probability that he's also talking on the phone on the drive to each job. He cannot be alone in his own thoughts, whether or not he views it that way.

When he gets home from work, there's more espresso before he talks on the phone some more. He may be calling a woman he is planning a date with or he may be calling Miles or Tamra or me. But he is most definitely on the phone.

"Does he do all this stuff because he can't be alone in his own head for five minutes?" Rena asked.

Miles and Shaun have been hinting that they will probably try to move out soon. Maybe within the next few years or even sooner. My dad also has a roommate that has become another family member, so he wouldn't completely be alone. My dad doesn't need to be coddled. But he hasn't been in a house without at least one of his kids since he got sober.

"I think that's why he's content to have Miles and Shaun living there and having a roommate or whoever," Rena told me. "I don't think he ever would want to be in the house by himself."

I asked my dad what he will do when Miles and Shaun move out. He said he'll sell the house and move somewhere smaller. It's weird hearing him say that. It reminds me of when my mom's mother discussed wanting to move out of her home to a small apartment when my grandpa died. It feels like something is dying.

"I'll be fine by myself," my dad said, reassuring himself and me.

My dad has been sober for 31 years. He has spent most of those years attending NA meetings, managing his hauling business and raising three children. He likes helping other people. NA has been such an essential part of my dad's life that Miles, Tamra and I have been to conventions with him.

Before the pandemic, my dad volunteered every month at a prison in San Diego, talking to inmates about his own experience in jail and prison. He allowed friends in recovery to stay in our house.

I told him that his life seems like it has been exhausting. It worries me even as I understand better. If he sits for just a moment, he wouldn't be who he is. The fabric of his being is embedded in his need to always be doing something. He needs the chaos, the hard work and the overly caffeinated habits he has picked up along the way.

My dad's parents have died. I asked him if he thought they would be proud to see the man and father he has become.

"I know they were proud when they passed away, they expressed it to me," he said, "considering where I went and where I got to – and

154 A PORTRAIT OF MY IMPERFECT FATHER

not because they did it. Through the miracle of recovery, I got it on my own. They realized I could sustain, I was taking care of business, I got a house and had kids. I didn't rely on them at all, economically, or anything else – I was successful."

THE DAUGHTER
WHO LIVED

Ragnhildur Thrastardottir

"They are three," he said, pointing to the water. The men on the other side of the river were eating lunch when the car went into the water. The driver had pulled him out but not his wife and daughters. The men eating their lunch offered to get help. But no one went back into the water.

They had been on an excursion. They had stopped to pick blueberries before continuing on to the waterfall Gullfoss in Haukadalur, on the south coast of Iceland.

The driver later told a reporter that he had to take a sharp turn to cross the bridge, but when he tried to slow down, he discovered that the brakes had failed. He tried to steer the car straight, but it plunged

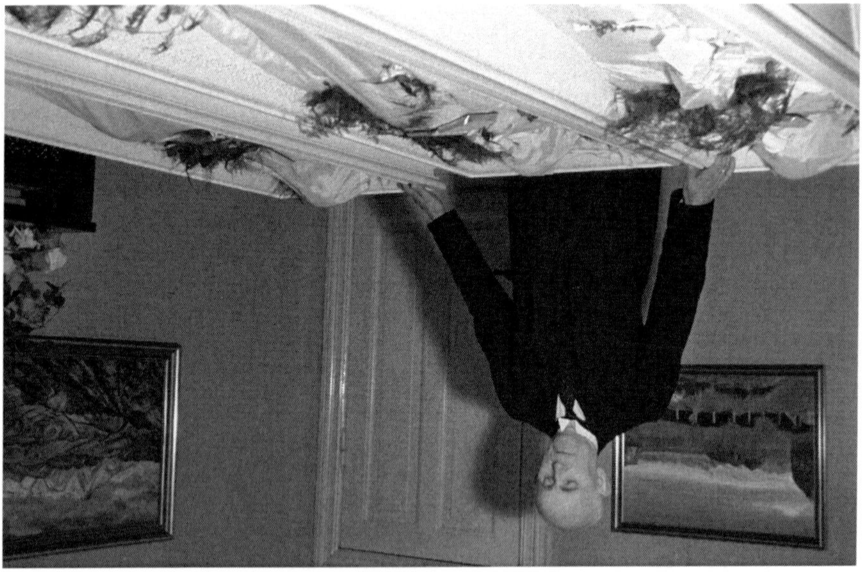

down a 40-foot embankment into the Tungufljót River.

The driver said he had rammed the window open to escape the car, and when he emerged, he saw the head of Sigurbjörn Gíslason, who had once hoped to become a priest but who had instead become a theologian. Sigurbjörn had married well, having taken as a wife Guðrún Lárusdóttir, who at 58 was a member of the Icelandic Parliament. They had four sons and three daughters, two of whom, along with their mother, were nowhere to be seen.

The call to the third daughter, Lára Sigurbjörnsdóttir, came later that afternoon. She lived in the east of Iceland with her husband, Ásgeir Einarsson, a veterinarian. They did not have a phone of their own, and so the call came to the telephone exchange in the nearby town of Egilsstaðir. The operator alerted a local teenager, and together they drove to tell Lára what had happened at the river. The messenger found them in a field threshing hay. The sound of her cry would stay with him for the rest of his long life.

Lára found someone to drive her to the north coast, where she boarded a ship to Reykjavik. She arrived home in time to see the bodies of her mother and sisters shrouded and white, lying in coffins in the living room.

Years later, she would tell one of her many granddaughters that for months after she moved into her father's house in Reykjavik, she sat in a chair and stared at nothing.

Lára's childhood home still stands on the West Side of Reykjavik. It's a two-story wooden house her parents built in 1906. It's called Ás. Lára's mother used to invite all sorts of people to the house when she worked for the city – poor people, vagrants and wealthy people, too. But when Lára returned, the house felt empty.

Lára had left the house, first to study in Denmark and then to become a schoolteacher in the east. She and Ásgeir married in 1937, even though her brothers warned her they wouldn't be a good fit. "You're just too different," they said. She'd been raised in a home tended by servants. His family lived in a house that barely fit them. She was raised by intellectuals and his parents were of the working class. He was so poor that he joined his school rowing team because they got free lunches.

He became a veterinarian for the state, responsible for an entire district. After the accident, however, he abandoned his practice to move to Reykjavik to join Lára, who would not leave her childhood home until a few weeks before her death when her family moved her to a nursing home.

Ásgeir could not find work as a veterinarian in Reykjavik, and Lára would not leave Ás and more importantly, her widowed father. In time Ásgeir had no choice but to take a job as a cab driver. This became a matter of some shame. "Your grandfather was nothing but a cab driver," one of his granddaughters would later recall her boss saying.

He drove a cab for seven years until he finally found work as a veterinarian a long drive away from Reykjavik. Ásgeir buried himself in work and was barely ever home.

"Maybe she felt like she could hold on to her mother by staying in Ás," says Guðrún, the eldest of Lára and Ásgeir's five children. "And then it became a fixed idea. She sacrificed herself for that house."

Guðrún was born in 1940, two years after the accident. She was given her grandmother's name, which was a burden in itself.

"It would be good if she stood up to the name," an aunt wrote to Lára after her Guðrún was born. "May she alleviate your harm and give you immense joy."

Guðrún is now 82 and always has a smile on her face. She's the sort of person who can't sit down when she's hosting a party because she wants to be sure everyone is happy.

When Ásgeir and Lára's daughters talk about the house, they smile slightly as they recall their childhoods there. They have long since moved away and avoid seeing the house. The family sold it in 2005, and it has since been renovated. But others in the family, such as Lára and Ásgeir's granddaughter María, are drawn to it.

One day she was taking a walk when she suddenly found herself in the garden by the house. Her grandmother had spent hours in the garden caring for the flowers and hosting guests. The new owner of the house invited her in.

The house was very different, inside and out. There were only three bedrooms instead of the seven she had known as a child. The kitchen walls had been torn down. Everything was brighter. "It was nice to see the changes," María later said. "But when I told my mother about them, she wasn't interested in visiting."

None of Lára and Ásgeir's daughters have returned to Ás.

"It's not my time there anymore," Guðrún says.

Her sister Sigrún agrees. "There's simply a new time playing out there now."

Yet to this day, they still call themselves the Ás-family.

One day in 1988, María was sitting by the front door of Ás. She had been spending the summer there, living with her grandparents. Lára had been traveling for a few days and was on her way back home from Denmark.

María had noticed her grandfather's excitement that morning. He was freshly shaved, and she could smell his cologne. He was smiling broadly as he stood by the front door waiting for Lára to return. María watched as the doorknob turned, and Ásgeir's smile widened. Lára walked in and stepped past him without saying a word. His smile faded away.

"It was actually his attitude that was unusual that day," María says. She had seldom seen her grandparents talk or even engage with one another. It had been that way for years. They had moved into separate bedrooms decades earlier.

Ásgeir would walk down the stairs in the morning and bid his wife good morning. Lára wouldn't respond. Years earlier, when their children were still living with them, they had started to use the children as messengers: "Tell your mother..." Ásgeir would begin. Lára would do the same.

"The first 25 years were good," Ásgeir once told his daughter Guðrún.

Ásgeir did not move out of the house until he was 85. He was still capable of caring for himself. Lára opposed his decision to move to a nursing home.

He got to shine in his new home. He knew everyone and spent his days chatting with the other residents. He read, took walks, sang and swam. He was respected and happy. His children visited him often. One day, he told his daughter Áslaug, "I fell in love with another woman."

The affair happened after he and Lára had been married for many years. The woman lived outside of Reykjavik. Áslaug listened to her father's story, nodding but asking no questions and feeling no anger.

Lára did learn of the affair and grew bitter. Áslaug would feel the bitterness in the frosty silence between her parents.

"Why don't you just get a divorce?" Guðrún later asked her mother.

"It's the house," Lára replied.

Lára worked as a teacher and occasionally as a tour guide for elderly Icelandic tourists in Mallorca. Her income was modest, and the house was big. Someone had to take care of it and share in the cost. She needed her husband's salary to make ends meet.

"I always reckoned you would move into Ás," Lára later told Guðrún. Her tone was hopeful.

"We can't do that," replied Guðrún, who was in her sixties at the time. "We're too old, and the house is filled with sorrow."

After Lára's death, Guðrún, who is a librarian and enthusiastic about file keeping, returned to Ás and made her way to the attic to begin sorting. She carried away boxes and boxes of Christmas cards, everyday notes, invoices, letters and photos. It took her months to sort through them. In the meantime, the house was sold. The passing of the house from the family saddened Guðrún. She kept emptying the house, room by room.

One day she was in her mother's bedroom. In the drawer of her bedside table, she found an old letter. The handwriting was hard to read. But as she read, she felt a chill.

It read: *"Dear mother, why were you taken from me?"* Lára had written the letter in 1938, after the accident. *"I just want to cry and cry by your side, but I know it's impossible. Your dear Lára is close to giving up."*

Guðrún was shocked to see her mother trying to write herself out of her grief. Yet as she read, she wondered, "Why didn't she just move back to her husband in the East?"

Lára's father, Sigurbjörn, died in 1969 – 31 years after the accident. And in those 31 years, Lára cooked his meals and cleaned his house. Even as she herself became a parent, she would not abandon her father. Nor, in the years after his death, would she abandon his home.

She would continue to take care of it, changing the tiles and repairing the linoleum in the bathroom. Still, there was one part of the house she avoided.

"Should we tidy up in the attic?" Guðrún sometimes asked her mother.

"Not now," Lára always replied.

She was 92 when, on the day before she was to undergo surgery for colon cancer, she finally climbed up to the attic to begin sorting through all the disorganized documents from herself, her children, her parents, and even their parents – memories that had piled up in the 100 years since her parents built Ás.

Lára approached the papers with care. Even though her mind was clear, the job was almost too much for her. Weak as she was, she tried to establish some order, perhaps hoping she would later have time to finish the work.

But after the surgery, she was too frail to return home. She had pleaded with her daughters to take care of her in Ás. But her daughters said they could not. "Not even you," she said to Guðrún.

María visited Lára in the nursing home a few days before she died. She watched as Lára stretched her hands into the air. It was as if Lára was trying to free something inside of herself.

"It would have been so good for my grandmother to move," María thought. "Not only out of that house but also into a reckoning with the past."

A few dozen people gathered at the river bank by Tungufljót, looking into the water where the car had plunged 80 years earlier. A few thought about the three women and how they were trapped in the back of the car as it sunk to the bottom. Yet both old and young watched as the river flowed on forward. They clutched red roses. Their children were playing close by, kicking stones and laughing. Everyone began to sing a hymn, the same one that the three women had sung in church the morning they died.

Drive out, O king of suns,
generous and great,
human every sorrow
from the fortress of the heart

They tossed their roses into the river and watched as the roses floated down with the stream and finally disappeared.

Made in United States
North Haven, CT
02 May 2023

36181910R00091